THE PELICAN SHAKESPEARE
GENERAL EDITORS

STEPHEN ORGEL
A. R. BRAUNMULLER

The First Part of Henry the Sixth

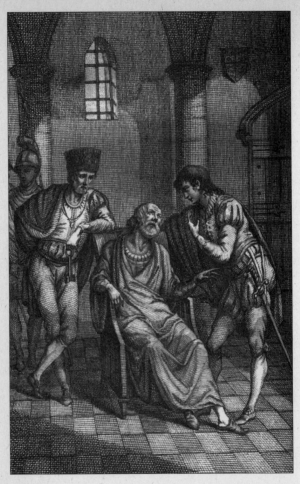

The death of Mortimer (II.5), frontispiece to the play
in Bell's Shakespeare, 1774, including a highly fanciful
version of medieval costume that reflects the growing interest
in period decor in the theater. The play had been popular
during the Restoration in an adaptation by John Crowne.
By 1774, however, it had not been performed for almost
a century, and the editorial note in Bell's edition says,
"It is not to be recommended for representation."

William Shakespeare

The First Part of
Henry the Sixth

EDITED BY WILLIAM MONTGOMERY
WITH AN INTRODUCTION BY JANIS LULL

PENGUIN BOOKS

PENGUIN BOOKS
Published by the Penguin Group
Penguin Putnam Inc., 375 Hudson Street,
New York, New York 10014, U.S.A.
Penguin Books Ltd, 27 Wrights Lane,
London W8 5TZ, England
Penguin Books Australia Ltd, Ringwood,
Victoria, Australia
Penguin Books Canada Ltd, 10 Alcorn Avenue,
Toronto, Ontario, Canada M4V 3B2
Penguin Books (N.Z.) Ltd, 182–190 Wairau Road,
Auckland 10, New Zealand

Penguin Books Ltd, Registered Offices:
Harmondsworth, Middlesex, England

The First Part of King Henry the Sixth edited by David Bevington
published in the United States of America in Penguin Books 1966
Revised edition published 1979
This new edition edited by William Montgomery with
an introduction by Janis Lull published 2000

1 3 5 7 9 10 8 6 4 2

Copyright © Penguin Books Inc., 1966
Copyright © Viking Penguin Inc., 1979
Copyright © Penguin Putnam Inc., 2000
All rights reserved

ISBN 0-14-07.1465 0
(CIP data available)

Printed in the United States of America
Set in Adobe Garamond
Designed by Virginia Norey

Contents

Publisher's Note

IT IS ALMOST half a century since the first volumes of the Pelican Shakespeare appeared under the general editorship of Alfred Harbage. The fact that a new edition, rather than simply a revision, has been undertaken reflects the profound changes textual and critical studies of Shakespeare have undergone in the past twenty years. For the new Pelican series, the texts of the plays and poems have been thoroughly revised in accordance with recent scholarship, and in some cases have been entirely reedited. New introductions and notes have been provided in all the volumes. But the new Shakespeare is also designed as a successor to the original series; the previous editions have been taken into account, and the advice of the previous editors has been solicited where it was feasible to do so.

Certain textual features of the new Pelican Shakespeare should be particularly noted. All lines are numbered that contain a word, phrase, or allusion explained in the glossarial notes. In addition, for convenience, every tenth line is also numbered, in italics when no annotation is indicated. The intrusive and often inaccurate place headings inserted by early editors are omitted (as is becoming standard practice), but for the convenience of those who miss them, an indication of locale now appears as the first item in the annotation of each scene.

In the interest of both elegance and utility, each speech prefix is set in a separate line when the speaker's lines are in verse, except when those words form the second half of a verse line. Thus the verse form of the speech is kept visually intact. What is printed as verse and what is printed as prose has, in general, the authority of the original texts. Departures from the original texts in this regard have only the authority of editorial tradition and the judgment of the Pelican editors; and, in a few instances, are admittedly arbitrary.

The Theatrical World

ECONOMIC REALITIES determined the theatrical world in which Shakespeare's plays were written, performed, and received. For centuries in England, the primary theatrical tradition was nonprofessional. Craft guilds (or "mysteries") provided religious drama – mystery plays – as part of the celebration of religious and civic festivals, and schools and universities staged classical and neoclassical drama in both Latin and English as part of their curricula. In these forms, drama was established and socially acceptable. Professional theater, in contrast, existed on the margins of society. The acting companies were itinerant; playhouses could be any available space – the great halls of the aristocracy, town squares, civic halls, inn yards, fair booths, or open fields – and income was sporadic, dependent on the passing of the hat or on the bounty of local patrons. The actors, moreover, were considered little better than vagabonds, constantly in danger of arrest or expulsion.

In the late 1560s and 1570s, however, English professional theater began to gain respectability. Wealthy aristocrats fond of drama – the Lord Admiral, for example, or the Lord Chamberlain – took acting companies under their protection so that the players technically became members of their households and were no longer subject to arrest as homeless or masterless men. Permanent theaters were first built at this time as well, allowing the companies to control and charge for entry to their performances.

Shakespeare's livelihood, and the stunning artistic explosion in which he participated, depended on pragmatic and architectural effort. Professional theater requires ways to restrict access to its offerings; if it does not, and admission fees cannot be charged, the actors do not get paid, the costumes go to a pawnbroker, and there is no such thing as a professional, ongoing theatrical tradition. The answer to that economic need arrived in the late 1560s and 1570s with the creation of the so-called public or amphitheater playhouse. Recent discoveries indicate that the precursor of the Globe playhouse in London (where Shakespeare's mature plays were presented) and the Rose theater (which presented Christopher Marlowe's plays and some of Shakespeare's earliest ones) was the Red Lion theater of 1567. Archaeological studies of the foundations of the Rose and Globe theaters have revealed that the open-air theater of the 1590s and later was probably a polygonal building with fourteen to twenty or twenty-four sides, multistoried, from 75 to 100 feet in diameter, with a raised, partly covered "thrust" stage that projected into a group of standing patrons, or "groundlings," and a covered gallery, seating up to 2,500 or more (very crowded) spectators.

These theaters might have been about half full on any given day, though the audiences were larger on holidays or when a play was advertised, as old and new were, through printed playbills posted around London. The metropolitan area's late-Tudor, early-Stuart population (circa 1590–1620) has been estimated at about 150,000 to 250,000. It has been supposed that in the mid-1590s there were about 15,000 spectators per week at the public theaters; thus, as many as 10 percent of the local population went to the theater regularly. Consequently, the theaters' repertories – the plays available for this experienced and frequent audience – had to change often: in the month between September 15 and October 15, 1595, for instance, the Lord Admiral's Men performed twenty-eight times in eighteen different plays.

Since natural light illuminated the amphitheaters' stages, performances began between noon and two o'clock and ran without a break for two or three hours. They often concluded with a jig, a fencing display, or some other nondramatic exhibition. Weather conditions determined the season for the amphitheaters: plays were performed every day (including Sundays, sometimes, to clerical dismay) except during Lent – the forty days before Easter – or periods of plague, or sometimes during the summer months when law courts were not in session and the most affluent members of the audience were not in London.

To a modern theatergoer, an amphitheater stage like that of the Rose or Globe would appear an unfamiliar mixture of plainness and elaborate decoration. Much of the structure was carved or painted, sometimes to imitate marble; elsewhere, as under the canopy projecting over the stage, to represent the stars and the zodiac. Appropriate painted canvas pictures (of Jerusalem, for example, if the play was set in that city) were apparently hung on the wall behind the acting area, and tragedies were accompanied by black hangings, presumably something like crepe festoons or bunting. Although these theaters did not employ what we would call scenery, early modern spectators saw numerous large props, such as the "bar" at which a prisoner stood during a trial, the "mossy bank" where lovers reclined, an arbor for amorous conversation, a chariot, gallows, tables, trees, beds, thrones, writing desks, and so forth. Audiences might learn a scene's location from a sign (reading "Athens," for example) carried across the stage (as in Bertolt Brecht's twentieth-century productions). Equally captivating (and equally irritating to the theater's enemies) were the rich costumes and personal props the actors used: the most valuable items in the surviving theatrical inventories are the swords, gowns, robes, crowns, and other items worn or carried by the performers.

Magic appealed to Shakespeare's audiences as much as it does to us today, and the theater exploited many deceptive and spectacular devices. A winch in the loft above the stage, called "the heavens," could lower and raise actors playing gods, goddesses, and other supernatural figures to and from the main acting area, just as one or more trapdoors permitted entrances and exits to and from the area, called "hell," beneath the stage. Actors wore elementary makeup such as wigs, false beards, and face paint, and they employed pig's bladders filled with animal blood to make wounds seem more real. They had rudimentary but effective ways of pretending to behead or hang a person. Supernumeraries (stagehands or actors not needed in a particular scene) could make thunder sounds (by shaking a metal sheet or rolling an iron ball down a chute) and show lightning (by blowing inflammable resin through tubes into a flame). Elaborate fireworks enhanced the effects of dragons flying through the air or imitated such celestial phenomena as comets, shooting stars, and multiple suns. Horses' hoofbeats, bells (located perhaps in the tower above the stage), trumpets and drums, clocks, cannon shots and gunshots, and the like were common sound effects. And the music of viols, cornets, oboes, and recorders was a regular feature of theatrical performances.

For two relatively brief spans, from the late 1570s to 1590 and from 1599 to 1614, the amphitheaters competed with the so-called private, or indoor, theaters, which originated as, or later represented themselves as, educational institutions training boys as singers for church services and court performances. These indoor theaters had two features that were distinct from the amphitheaters': their personnel and their playing spaces. The amphitheaters' adult companies included both adult men, who played the male roles, and boys, who played the female roles; the private, or indoor, theater companies, on the other hand, were entirely composed of boys aged about 8 to 16, who were, or could pretend to be, candidates for singers in a church or a royal boys' choir. (Until 1660, professional theatrical companies included no women.) The playing space would appear much more familiar to modern audiences than the long-vanished amphitheaters; the later indoor theaters were, in fact, the ancestors of the typical modern theater. They were enclosed spaces, usually rectangular, with the stage filling one end of the rectangle and the audience arrayed in seats or benches across (and sometimes lining) the building's longer axis. These spaces staged plays less frequently than the public theaters (perhaps only once a week) and held far fewer spectators than the amphitheaters: about 200 to 600, as opposed to 2,500 or more. Fewer patrons mean a smaller gross income, unless each pays more. Not surprisingly, then, private theaters charged higher prices than the amphitheaters, probably sixpence, as opposed to a penny for the cheapest entry.

Protected from the weather, the indoor theaters presented plays later in the day than the amphitheaters, and used artificial illumination – candles in sconces or candelabra. But candles melt, and need replacing, snuffing, and trimming, and these practical requirements may have been part of the reason the indoor theaters introduced breaks in the performance, the intermission so dear to the heart of theatergoers and to the pocketbooks of theater concessionaires ever since. Whether motivated by the need to tend to the candles or by the entrepreneurs' wishing to sell oranges and liquor, or both, the indoor theaters eventually established the modern convention of the non-continuous performance. In the early modern "private" theater, musical performances apparently filled the intermissions, which in Stuart theater jargon seem to have been called "acts."

At the end of the first decade of the seventeenth century, the distinction between public amphitheaters and private indoor companies ceased. For various cultural, political, and economic reasons, individual companies gained control of both the public, open-air theaters and the indoor ones, and companies mixing adult men and boys took over the formerly "private" theaters. Despite the death of the boys' companies and of their highly innovative theaters (for which such luminous playwrights as Ben Jonson, George Chapman, and John Marston wrote), their playing spaces and conventions had an immense impact on subsequent plays: not merely for the intervals (which stressed the artistic and architectonic importance of "acts"), but also because they introduced political and social satire as a popular dramatic ingredient, even in tragedy, and a wider range of actorly effects, encouraged by their more intimate playing spaces.

Even the briefest sketch of the Shakespearean theatrical world would be incomplete without some comment on the social and cultural dimensions of theaters and playing in the period. In an intensely hierarchical and status-conscious society, professional actors and their ventures had hardly any respectability; as we have indicated, to protect themselves against laws designed to curb vagabondage and the increase of masterless men, actors resorted to the near-fiction that they were the servants of noble masters, and wore their distinctive livery. Hence the company for which Shakespeare wrote in the 1590s called itself the Lord Chamberlain's Men and pretended that the public, money-getting performances were in fact rehearsals for private performances before that high court official. From 1598, the Privy Council had licensed theatrical companies, and after 1603, with the accession of King James I, the companies gained explicit royal protection, just as the Queen's Men had for a time under Queen Elizabeth. The Chamberlain's Men became the King's Men, and the other companies were patronized by the other members of the royal family.

These designations were legal fictions that half-concealed an important economic and social development, the evolution away from the theater's organization on the model of the guild, a self-regulating confraternity of individual artisans, into a proto-capitalist organization. Shakespeare's company became a joint-stock company, where persons who supplied capital and, in some cases, such as Shakespeare's, capital and talent, employed themselves and others in earning a return on that capital. This development meant that actors and theater companies were outside both the traditional guild structures, which required some form of civic or royal charter, and the feudal household organization of master-and-servant. This anomalous, maverick social and economic condition made theater companies practically unruly and potentially even dangerous; consequently, numerous official bodies – including the London metropolitan and ecclesiastical authorities as well as, occasionally, the royal court itself – tried, without much success, to control and even to disband them.

Public officials had good reason to want to close the theaters: they were attractive nuisances – they drew often riotous crowds, they were always noisy, and they could be politically offensive and socially insubordinate. Until the Civil War, however, anti-theatrical forces failed to shut down professional theater, for many reasons – limited surveillance and few police powers, tensions or outright hostilities among the agencies that sought to check or channel theatrical activity, and lack of clear policies for control. Another reason must have been the theaters' undeniable popularity. Curtailing any activity enjoyed by such a substantial percentage of the population was difficult, as various Roman emperors attempting to limit circuses had learned, and the Tudor-Stuart audience was not merely large, it was socially diverse and included women. The prevalence of public entertainment in this period has been underestimated. In fact, fairs, holidays, games, sporting events, the equivalent of modern parades, freak shows, and street exhibitions all abounded, but the theater was the most widely and frequently available entertainment to which people of every class had access. That fact helps account both for its quantity and for the fear and anger it aroused.

WILLIAM SHAKESPEARE OF
STRATFORD-UPON-AVON, GENTLEMAN

Many people have said that we know very little about William Shakespeare's life – pinheads and postcards are often mentioned as appropriately tiny surfaces on which to record the available information. More imaginatively and perhaps more correctly, Ralph Waldo Emerson wrote, "Shakespeare is the only biographer of Shakespeare. . . . So far from Shakespeare's being the least known, he is the one person in all modern history fully known to us."

In fact, we know more about Shakespeare's life than we do about almost any other English writer's of his era. His last will and testament (dated March 25, 1616) survives, as do numerous legal contracts and court documents involving Shakespeare as principal or witness, and parish records in Stratford and London. Shakespeare appears quite often in official records of King James's royal court, and of course Shakespeare's name appears on numerous title pages and in the written and recorded words of his literary contemporaries Robert Greene, Henry Chettle, Francis Meres, John Davies of Hereford, Ben Jonson, and many others. Indeed, if we make due allowance for the bloating of modern, run-of-the-mill bureaucratic records, more information has survived over the past four hundred years about William Shakespeare of Stratford-upon-Avon, Warwickshire, than is likely to survive in the next four hundred years about any reader of these words.

What we do not have are entire categories of information – Shakespeare's private letters or diaries, drafts and revisions of poems and plays, critical prefaces or essays, commendatory verse for other writers' works, or instructions guiding his fellow actors in their performances, for instance – that we imagine would help us understand and appreciate his surviving writings. For all we know, many such data never existed as written records. Many literary and theatrical critics, not knowing what might once have existed, more or less cheerfully accept the situation; some even make a theoretical virtue of it by claiming that such data are irrelevant to understanding and interpreting the plays and poems.

So, what do we know about William Shakespeare, the man responsible for thirty-seven or perhaps more plays, more than 150 sonnets, two lengthy narrative poems, and some shorter poems?

While many families by the name of Shakespeare (or some variant spelling) can be identified in the English Midlands as far back as the twelfth century, it seems likely that the dramatist's grandfather, Richard, moved to Snitterfield, a town not far from Stratford-upon-Avon, sometime before 1529. In Snitterfield, Richard Shakespeare leased farmland from the very wealthy Robert Arden. By 1552, Richard's son John had moved to a large house on Henley Street in Stratford-upon-Avon, the house that stands today as "The Birthplace." In Stratford, John Shakespeare traded as a glover, dealt in wool, and lent money at interest; he also served in a variety of civic posts, including "High Bailiff," the municipality's equivalent of mayor. In 1557, he married Robert Arden's youngest daughter, Mary. Mary and John had four sons – William was the oldest – and four daughters, of whom only Joan outlived her most celebrated sibling. William was baptized (an event entered in the Stratford parish church records) on April 26, 1564, and it has become customary, without any good factual support, to suppose he was born on April 23, which happens to be the feast day of Saint George, patron saint of England, and is also the date on which he died, in 1616. Shakespeare married Anne Hathaway in 1582, when he was eighteen and she was twenty-six; their first child was born five months later. It has been generally assumed that the marriage was enforced and subsequently unhappy, but these are only assumptions; it has been estimated, for instance, that up to one third of Elizabethan brides were pregnant when they married. Anne and William Shakespeare had three children: Susanna, who married a prominent local physician, John Hall; and the twins Hamnet, who died young in 1596, and Judith, who married Thomas Quiney – apparently a rather shady individual. The name Hamnet was unusual but not unique: he and his twin sister were named for their godparents, Shakespeare's neighbors Hamnet and Judith Sadler. Shakespeare's father died in 1601 (the year of *Hamlet*), and Mary Arden Shakespeare died in 1608 (the year of *Coriolanus*). William Shakespeare's last surviving direct descendant was his granddaughter Elizabeth Hall, who died in 1670.

Between the birth of the twins in 1585 and a clear reference to Shakespeare as a practicing London dramatist in Robert Greene's sensationalizing, satiric pamphlet, *Greene's Groatsworth of Wit* (1592), there is no record of where William Shakespeare was or what he was doing. These seven so-called lost years have been imaginatively filled by scholars and other students of Shakespeare: some think he traveled to Italy, or fought in the Low Countries, or studied law or medicine, or worked as an apprentice actor/writer, and so on to even more fanciful possibilities. Whatever the biographical facts for those "lost" years, Greene's nasty remarks in 1592 testify to professional envy and to the fact that Shakespeare already had a successful career in London. Speaking to his fellow playwrights, Greene warns both generally and specifically:

> . . . trust them [actors] not: for there is an upstart crow, beautified with our feathers, that with his tiger's heart wrapped in a player's hide supposes he is as well able to bombast out a blank verse as the best of you; and being an absolute Johannes Factotum, is in his own conceit the only Shake-scene in a country.

The passage mimics a line from *3 Henry VI* (hence the play must have been performed before Greene wrote) and seems to say that "Shake-scene" is both actor and play-wright, a jack-of-all-trades. That same year, Henry Chettle protested Greene's remarks in *Kind-Heart's Dream,* and each of the next two years saw the publication of poems – *Venus and Adonis* and *The Rape of Lucrece,* respectively – publicly ascribed to (and dedicated by) Shakespeare. Early in 1595 he was named one of the senior members of a prominent acting company, the Lord Chamberlain's Men, when they received payment for court performances during the 1594 Christmas season.

Clearly, Shakespeare had achieved both success and reputation in London. In 1596, upon Shakespeare's application, the College of Arms granted his father the now-familiar coat of arms he had taken the first steps to obtain almost twenty years before, and in 1598, John's son – now permitted to call himself "gentleman" – took a 10 percent share in the new Globe playhouse. In 1597, he bought a substantial bourgeois house, called New Place, in Stratford – the garden remains, but Shakespeare's house, several times rebuilt, was torn down in 1759 – and over the next few years Shakespeare spent large sums buying land and making other investments in the town and its environs. Though he worked in London, his family remained in Stratford, and he seems always to have considered Stratford the home he would eventually return to. Something approaching a disinterested appreciation of Shakespeare's popular and professional status appears in Francis Meres's *Palladis Tamia* (1598), a not especially imaginative and perhaps therefore persuasive record of literary reputations. Reviewing contemporary English writers, Meres lists the titles of many of Shakespeare's plays, including one not now known, *Love's Labor's Won,* and praises his "mellifluous & hony-tongued" "sugred Sonnets," which were then circulating in manuscript (they were first collected in 1609). Meres describes Shakespeare as "one of the best" English playwrights of both comedy and tragedy. In *Remains . . . Concerning Britain* (1605),

William Camden – a more authoritative source than the imitative Meres – calls Shakespeare one of the "most pregnant witts of these our times" and joins him with such writers as Chapman, Daniel, Jonson, Marston, and Spenser. During the first decades of the seventeenth century, publishers began to attribute numerous play quartos, including some non-Shakespearean ones, to Shakespeare, either by name or initials, and we may assume that they deemed Shakespeare's name and supposed authorship, true or false, commercially attractive.

For the next ten years or so, various records show Shakespeare's dual career as playwright and man of the theater in London, and as an important local figure in Stratford. In 1608-9 his acting company – designated the "King's Men" soon after King James had succeeded Queen Elizabeth in 1603 – rented, refurbished, and opened a small interior playing space, the Blackfriars theater, in London, and Shakespeare was once again listed as a substantial sharer in the group of proprietors of the playhouse. By May 11, 1612, however, he describes himself as a Stratford resident in a London lawsuit – an indication that he had withdrawn from day-to-day professional activity and returned to the town where he had always had his main financial interests. When Shakespeare bought a substantial residential building in London, the Blackfriars Gatehouse, close to the theater of the same name, on March 10, 1613, he is recorded as William Shakespeare "of Stratford upon Avon in the county of Warwick, gentleman," and he named several London residents as the building's trustees. Still, he continued to participate in theatrical activity: when the new Earl of Rutland needed an allegorical design to bear as a shield, or *impresa,* at the celebration of King James's Accession Day, March 24, 1613, the earl's accountant recorded a payment of 44 shillings to Shakespeare for the device with its motto.

For the last few years of his life, Shakespeare evidently

concentrated his activities in the town of his birth. Most of the final records concern business transactions in Stratford, ending with the notation of his death on April 23, 1616, and burial in Holy Trinity Church, Stratford-upon-Avon.

THE QUESTION OF AUTHORSHIP

The history of ascribing Shakespeare's plays (the poems do not come up so often) to someone else began, as it continues, peculiarly. The earliest published claim that someone else wrote Shakespeare's plays appeared in an 1856 article by Delia Bacon in the American journal *Putnam's Monthly* – although an Englishman, Thomas Wilmot, had shared his doubts in private (even secretive) conversations with friends near the end of the eighteenth century. Bacon's was a sad personal history that ended in madness and poverty, but the year after her article, she published, with great difficulty and the bemused assistance of Nathaniel Hawthorne (then United States Consul in Liverpool, England), her *Philosophy of the Plays of Shakspere Unfolded.* This huge, ornately written, confusing farrago is almost unreadable; sometimes its intents, to say nothing of its arguments, disappear entirely beneath near-raving, ecstatic writing. Tumbled in with much supposed "philosophy" appear the claims that Francis Bacon (from whom Delia Bacon eventually claimed descent), Walter Ralegh, and several other contemporaries of Shakespeare's had written the plays. The book had little impact except as a ridiculed curiosity.

Once proposed, however, the issue gained momentum among people whose conviction was the greater in proportion to their ignorance of sixteenth- and seventeenth-century English literature, history, and society. Another American amateur, Catherine P. Ashmead Windle, made the next influential contribution to the cause when she published *Report to the British Museum* (1882), wherein she promised to open "the Cipher of Francis Bacon," though what she mostly offers, in the words of S. Schoenbaum, is "demented allegorizing." An entire new cottage industry grew from Windle's suggestion that the texts contain hidden, cryptographically discoverable ciphers – "clues" – to their authorship; and today there are not only books devoted to the putative ciphers, but also pamphlets, journals, and newsletters.

Although Baconians have led the pack of those seeking a substitute Shakespeare, in *"Shakespeare" Identified* (1920), J. Thomas Looney became the first published "Oxfordian" when he proposed Edward de Vere, seventeenth earl of Oxford, as the secret author of Shakespeare's plays. Also for Oxford and his "authorship" there are today dedicated societies, articles, journals, and books. Less popular candidates – Queen Elizabeth and Christopher Marlowe among them – have had adherents, but the movement seems to have divided into two main contending factions, Baconian and Oxfordian. (For further details on all the candidates for "Shakespeare," see S. Schoenbaum, *Shakespeare's Lives,* 2nd ed., 1991.)

The Baconians, the Oxfordians, and supporters of other candidates have one trait in common – they are snobs. Every pro-Bacon or pro-Oxford tract sooner or later claims that the historical William Shakespeare of Stratford-upon-Avon could not have written the plays because he could not have had the training, the university education, the experience, and indeed the imagination or background their author supposedly possessed. Only a learned genius like Bacon or an aristocrat like Oxford could have written such fine plays. (As it happens, lucky male children of the middle class had access to better education than most aristocrats in Elizabethan England – and Oxford was not particularly well educated.) Shakespeare received in the Stratford grammar school a formal education that would daunt many college graduates today; and popular rival playwrights such as the very learned Ben Jonson and George Chapman, both of whom also lacked university training, achieved great artistic success, without being taken as Bacon or Oxford.

Besides snobbery, one other quality characterizes the authorship controversy: lack of evidence. A great deal of testimony from Shakespeare's time shows that Shakespeare wrote Shakespeare's plays and that his contemporaries recognized them as distinctive and distinctly superior. (Some of that contemporary evidence is collected in E. K. Chambers, *William Shakespeare: A Study of Facts and Problems*, 2 vols., 1930.) Since that testimony comes from Shakespeare's enemies and theatrical competitors as well as from his co-workers and from the Elizabethan equivalent of literary journalists, it seems unlikely that, if any of these sources had known he was a fraud, they would have failed to record that fact.

Books About Shakespeare's Theater

Useful scholarly studies of theatrical life in Shakespeare's day include: G. E. Bentley, *The Jacobean and Caroline Stage*, 7 vols. (1941-68), and the same author's *The Professions of Dramatist and Player in Shakespeare's Time, 1590-1642* (1986); E. K. Chambers, *The Elizabethan Stage*, 4 vols. (1923); R. A. Foakes, *Illustrations of the English Stage, 1580-1642* (1985); Andrew Gurr, *The Shakespearean Stage*, 3rd ed. (1992), and the same author's *Play-going in Shakespeare's London*, 2nd ed. (1996); Edwin Nungezer, *A Dictionary of Actors* (1929); Carol Chillington Rutter, ed., *Documents of the Rose Playhouse* (1984).

Books About Shakespeare's Life

The following books provide scholarly, documented accounts of Shakespeare's life: G. E. Bentley, *Shakespeare: A Biographical Handbook* (1961); E. K. Chambers, *William Shakespeare: A Study of Facts and Problems*, 2 vols. (1930); S. Schoenbaum, *William Shakespeare: A Compact*

Documentary Life (1977); and *Shakespeare's Lives,* 2nd ed. (1991), by the same author. Many scholarly editions of Shakespeare's complete works print brief compilations of essential dates and events. References to Shakespeare's works up to 1700 are collected in C. M. Ingleby et al., *The Shakespeare Allusion-Book,* rev. ed., 2 vols. (1932).

The Texts of Shakespeare

As FAR AS WE KNOW, only one manuscript conceivably in Shakespeare's own hand may (and even this is much disputed) exist: a few pages of a play called *Sir Thomas More,* which apparently was never performed. What we do have, as later readers, performers, scholars, students, are printed texts. The earliest of these survive in two forms: quartos and folios. Quartos (from the Latin for "four") are small books, printed on sheets of paper that were then folded in fours, to make eight double-sided pages. When these were bound together, the result was a squarish, eminently portable volume that sold for the relatively small sum of sixpence (translating in modern terms to about $5.00). In folios, on the other hand, the sheets are folded only once, in half, producing large, impressive volumes taller than they are wide. This was the format for important works of philosophy, science, theology, and literature (the major precedent for a folio Shakespeare was Ben Jonson's *Works,* 1616). The decision to print the works of a popular playwright in folio is an indication of how far up on the social scale the theatrical profession had come during Shakespeare's lifetime. The Shakespeare folio was an expensive book, selling for between fifteen and eighteen shillings, depending on the binding (in modern terms, from about $150 to $180). Twenty Shakespeare plays of the thirty-seven that survive first appeared in quarto, seventeen of which appeared during Shakespeare's lifetime; the rest of the plays are found only in folio.

The First Folio was published in 1623, seven years after Shakespeare's death, and was authorized by his fellow actors, the co-owners of the King's Men. This publication was certainly a mark of the company's enormous respect for Shakespeare; but it was also a way of turning the old plays, most of which were no longer current in the playhouse, into ready money (the folio includes only Shakespeare's plays, not his sonnets or other nondramatic verse). Whatever the motives behind the publication of the folio, the texts it preserves constitute the basis for almost all later editions of the playwright's works. The texts, however, differ from those of the earlier quartos, sometimes in minor respects but often significantly – most strikingly in the two texts of *King Lear,* but also in important ways in *Hamlet, Othello,* and *Troilus and Cressida.* (The variants are recorded in the textual notes to each play in the new Pelican series.) The differences in these texts represent, in a sense, the essence of theater: the texts of plays were initially not intended for publication. They were scripts, designed for the actors to perform – the principal life of the play at this period was in performance. And it follows that in Shakespeare's theater the playwright typically had no say either in how his play was performed or in the disposition of his text – he was an employee of the company. The authoritative figures in the theatrical enterprise were the shareholders in the company, who were for the most part the major actors. They decided what plays were to be done; they hired the playwright and often gave him an outline of the play they wanted him to write. Often, too, the play was a collaboration: the company would retain a group of writers, and parcel out the scenes among them. The resulting script was then the property of the company, and the actors would revise it as they saw fit during the course of putting it on stage. The resulting text belonged to the company. The playwright had no rights in it once he had been paid. (This system survives largely intact in the movie industry, and most of the playwrights of Shakespeare's time were as anonymous as most screenwriters are today.) The script could also, of course, continue to change as the tastes of audiences and the requirements of the actors changed. Many – perhaps most – plays were revised when they were reintroduced after any substantial absence from the repertory, or when they were performed by a company different from the one that originally commissioned the play.

Shakespeare was an exceptional figure in this world because he was not only a shareholder and actor in his company, but also its leading playwright – he was literally his own boss. He had, moreover, little interest in the publication of his plays, and even those that appeared during his lifetime with the authorization of the company show no signs of any editorial concern on the part of the author. Theater was, for Shakespeare, a fluid and supremely responsive medium – the very opposite of the great classic canonical text that has embodied his works since 1623.

The very fluidity of the original texts, however, has meant that Shakespeare has always had to be edited. Here is an example of how problematic the editorial project inevitably is, a passage from the most famous speech in *Romeo and Juliet,* Juliet's balcony soliloquy beginning "O Romeo, Romeo, wherefore art thou Romeo?" Since the eighteenth century, the standard modern text has read,

> What's Montague? It is nor hand, nor foot,
> Nor arm, nor face, nor any other part
> Belonging to a man. O be some other name!
> What's in a name? That which we call a rose
> By any other name would smell as sweet.
>   (II.2.40-44)

Editors have three early texts of this play to work from, two quarto texts and the folio. Here is how the First Quarto (1597) reads:

> Whats *Mountague?* It is nor hand nor foote,
> Nor arme, nor face, nor any other part.
> Whats in a name? That which we call a Rofe,
> By any other name would fmell as fweet:

Here is the Second Quarto (1599):

> Whats *Mountague?* it is nor hand nor foote,
> Nor arme nor face, ô be fome other name
> Belonging to a man.
> Whats in a name that which we call a rofe,
> By any other word would fmell as fweete,

And here is the First Folio (1623):

> What's *Mountague?* it is nor hand nor foote,
> Nor arme, nor face, O be fome other name
> Belonging to a man.
> What? in a names that which we call a Rofe,
> By any other word would fmell as fweete,

There is in fact no early text that reads as our modern text does – and this is the most famous speech in the play. Instead, we have three quite different texts, all of which are clearly some version of the same speech, but none of which seems to us a final or satisfactory version. The transcendently beautiful passage in modern editions is an editorial invention: editors have succeeded in conflating and revising the three versions into something we recognize as great poetry. Is this what Shakespeare "really" wrote? Who can say? What we can say is that Shakespeare always had performance, not a book, in mind.

Books About the Shakespeare Texts

The standard study of the printing history of the First Folio is W. W. Greg, *The Shakespeare First Folio* (1955). J. K. Walton, *The Quarto Copy for the First Folio of Shakespeare*

(1971), is a useful survey of the relation of the quartos to the folio. The second edition of Charlton Hinman's *Norton Facsimile* of the First Folio (1996), with a new introduction by Peter Blayney, is indispensable. Stanley Wells, Gary Taylor, John Jowett, and William Montgomery, *William Shakespeare: A Textual Companion,* keyed to the Oxford text, gives a comprehensive survey of the editorial situation for all the plays and poems.

THE GENERAL EDITORS

Introduction

IN A PAMPHLET printed in 1592 called *Pierce Penilesse His Supplication to the Divell,* Thomas Nashe praises a play that is almost certainly Shakespeare's *1 Henry VI:* "How would it have joyed brave Talbot (the terror of the French) to think that after he had lain two hundred years in his tomb, he should triumph again on the stage, and have his bones new embalmed with the tears of ten thousand spectators at least (at several times)." If Nashe's account is correct, the play enjoyed a huge success with Elizabethan audiences. In our own time, however, all three of Shakespeare's plays about the reign of Henry VI have been overshadowed by other works, such as *Richard III* and *Henry V,* in which strong protagonists transform English history into dramas of individual psychology. In contrast to some of these more famous Shakespearean histories, the Henry VI plays represent their title character as an uncertainty at the heart of the drama rather than a central figure. Instead of showing how historical circumstances emanate from the monarch's character, these works highlight the interdependence of character and circumstance.

Henry VI came to the throne when he was nine months old. The king's personality was thus shaped by public events, perhaps much more than events were ever shaped by the king. This certainly seems to be the assumption of Shakespeare's plays, which show Henry developing under the influence of politicians trying to use him instead of caretakers seeking to nurture him. In *1 Henry VI,* the king is absent entirely from the first two acts, which consist of a series of scenes juxtaposing the English wars in France with the strife among leaders at home. The play opens with the funeral of Henry V, and the shadow of that hero-king continues to reign in the first scene. His brother, Humphrey of Gloucester, eulogizes him as the best – indeed the only – monarch of English history:

> England ne'er had a king until his time.
> Virtue he had, deserving to command.
> His brandished sword did blind men with his
>   beams.
> His arms spread wider than a dragon's wings.
> His sparkling eyes, replete with wrathful fire,
> More dazzled and drove back his enemies
> Than midday sun, fierce bent against their faces.
> What should I say? His deeds exceed all speech.
> He ne'er lift up his hand but conquerèd.
>
>   (I.1.8–16)

Young Henry VI has no chance of growing up to be such a king. The untimely death of the father has left the son without a tutor and guide in the perilous life he must lead. For comparison, Shakespeare offers glimpses throughout the play of other children, with fathers. These include the French master gunner with his loyal son, Lord Talbot with the equally valiant John Talbot, Joan la Pucelle (which can mean either "Joan the maiden" or "Joan the whore") with the shepherd father she denies, and Margaret with the ambitious "king" René. Each of these children is more fortunate than Henry VI, if only in having a living father to revere or reject. Even York, whose discontent grows partly from his father's execution by Henry V, finds a substitute in his dying uncle Mortimer, who blesses York's quest for the crown.

Only Gloucester, the Lord Protector, has the potential to stand as a father figure for Henry, but he cannot sustain the boy because he cannot control his temper around the king's other advisers, especially the scheming Bishop of Winchester. These two nobles, quarreling at their first appearance together, show the audience immediate evidence of the plotting and dissension at the English court. Messengers begin to arrive with news of defeat in France, the first one speaking as a chorus to reveal the real causes of England's military collapse:

> No treachery, but want of men and money.
> Amongst the soldiers this is mutterèd:
> That here you maintain several factions,
> And whilst a field should be dispatched and fought,
> You are disputing of your generals.
>
> (I.1.69-73)

After the first scene, the action moves back and forth between the English wars in France and court disputes in England. In either setting, Henry VI is present only as a title, evoked by those who would assert their own political power. Lord Talbot, a chivalric hero in the mold of Henry V, does not fight the French in the name of the English king, but in his own. As one of Talbot's soldiers says, "The cry of 'Talbot' serves me for a sword, / For I have loaden me with many spoils, / Using no other weapon but his name" (II.1.81-83). On the domestic front, Henry's nobles fill the vacuum of his absence with ambitious plotting. When the king finally does make an entrance, at the start of Act III, he says nothing for several minutes while Gloucester, Winchester, and the other lords quarrel.

Shakespeare does not specify the king's age in *1 Henry VI,* but Warwick explicitly refers to him as a child (III.1.136), and Henry's first words to his wrangling uncles sound a child's pleading note:

> I would prevail, if prayers might prevail,
> To join your hearts in love and amity.
> O, what a scandal is it to our crown
> That two such noble peers as ye should jar!

> Believe me, lords, my tender years can tell
> Civil dissension is a viperous worm
> That gnaws the bowels of the commonwealth.
>   (68-74)

This opening speech makes it clear that the king has already been shaped by the negative influences around him: defeat, manipulation, neglect. He is an idealistic child who perceives his elders' mismanagement but can think of no solutions except prayers and homilies. His natural piety is baffled by the hypocrisy of his great-uncle, the Bishop of Winchester:

> Fie, uncle Beaufort! I have heard you preach
> That malice was a great and grievous sin;
> And will not you maintain the thing you teach,
> But prove a chief offender in the same?
>   (130-33)

The boy's awakening grasp of statecraft is no match for the fury of civil discord. As one partisan says, "if we be forbidden stones, we'll fall to it with our teeth" (92-93). In the end, even Henry's adolescent sexuality is ruthlessly manipulated by Suffolk, who seduces him into a marriage with Margaret of Anjou. The king has no adult support in his own court, not even from the "good" Duke Humphrey, a sign that England is failing to protect its infant king or to fashion him into a fit leader.

Except in this negative way, *1 Henry VI* has no main character, and certainly no hero. Characters of principle, such as Talbot and Gloucester, are impractical. Practical characters – Joan la Pucelle, Plantagenet, Suffolk – subscribe to no principle. The women in the play, like the men, want power, and like the men, they take different approaches to it. La Pucelle and the Bishop of Winchester show an unscrupulous drive for dominion. The Countess of Auvergne, like Richard Plantagenet, wavers between ambition and self-preservation, while Margaret of Anjou shows signs of both Joan's will to power and the countess's cunning. If the women use sex to gain ascendancy, the men, who control public life, are susceptible to such strategies. If the men – the dauphin, for example, or Suffolk – trade power for sex, the women seem eager to make such trades.

Even the heroic Talbot, who maintains his guard along with his courtesy, professes himself "not offended" (II.3.76) by the scheming Countess of Auvergne. As both Talbot and the countess seem to acknowledge, courtesy itself prescribes a power bargain between the genders. The hero puts himself under the lady's domestic authority in order, as Talbot says, to "Taste of your wine and see what cates you have" (79). The countess and Talbot both try to tip the balance, she by plotting to capture him, he by bringing along his army, just in case. Once the countess admits Talbot's superior force, however, equilibrium returns, no one is offended, and courtesy proceeds as usual. Like Talbot, the lady is aspiring and patriotic, but unlike him, she knows when to quit. For these qualities, brief as her appearance is, the countess should probably be seen if not as a positive figure, at least as one of the best politicians in the play.

Although much of *1 Henry VI* derives from the chronicle histories of Edward Hall (1548) and Raphael Holinshed (1587), the scene in which the Countess of Auvergne appears, II.3, is fictitious, as are the scenes before and after it. Such mingling of fact and fiction is typical of Shakespeare's method in the English history plays, as he converts his narrative sources into drama. The composite structure of *1 Henry VI* allows Shakespeare to suggest thematic comparisons and parallels between apparently unconnected events. The playwright uses incidents from the chronicle sources – the French victory at Orléans, for example – when they serve his dramatic purposes. On the other hand, he invents episodes, including an unhistorical English victory to parallel that of the French (II.1), when his comparative method requires them. *1 Henry VI* consists primarily of a series of emblematic displays, each scene juxtaposed meaningfully with the ones before and after it, with the implied connections left for spectators to complete in their own minds. Shakespeare gives us no chorus or narrator to explain why the action switches between England and France or why the play concentrates on the king's nobles and generals rather than on the king. We must see for ourselves how the bickering and neglect of Henry's "guardians" reveal both his stunted personality and its causes or how what happens in France helps explain what happens at home, and vice versa.

During the English defeat at Orléans, Talbot finds himself unable to beat Joan at hand-to-hand combat, and he experiences some uncharacteristic confusion:

My thoughts are whirlèd like a potter's wheel.
I know not where I am nor what I do.
A witch by fear, not force, like Hannibal
Drives back our troops and conquers as she lists.
(I.7.19-22)

Neither Talbot nor a reader of Shakespeare's text can tell whether Joan has escaped his wrath and scattered his army by witchcraft, psychological intimidation, or superior skill. Onstage, directors may make choices that favor one or another of these options, but the ambiguity of the scene as written suggests that the sources of Joan's power remain obscure to Talbot. Certainly the play does not insist that Joan prevails by sorcery. In fact, when we finally see her conjuring demons – "Help me this once" (V.3.12) – they refuse. Instead, the play implies that Talbot has been stopped by forces too sophisticated for the old-fashioned ideals that guide his chivalric behavior. Joan has won her place at the dauphin's side by a combination of myth-making, ambition, sexuality, and courage. She is willing to use all her powers, including physical and psychological seduction, to get ahead. Against such a multifaceted adversary, Talbot, the single-minded soldier, feels outmatched.

In retaking Orléans, however, Talbot reasserts the strength he had lost in the presence of La Pucelle. There follows the invented episode (II.2-3) in which the struggle between Talbot and Joan is reflected in the one between Talbot and the countess. In each case, Talbot wins when he relies on his competence as a leader of men. He is a military hero, at his best when heading up his army. He can be overcome, however, when war becomes an extension of psychological and political motives rather than a pure contest of honor and might. Talbot's temporary victories at Orléans and at the countess's castle foreshadow his final defeat; he is let down by English politicians, York (Plantagenet) and Somerset, rather than by personal weakness.

Two more incidents – the "Temple garden" scene (II.4), in which the Wars of the Roses begin with a law students' argument, and the scene in which Richard Plantagenet visits Mortimer in prison (II.5) – complete the central, fictitious section of the play. The quarrel between Plantagenet, who plucks a white rose, and Somerset, who takes a red one, originates in some point of law regarding Plantagenet's descent from Edward III. Plantagenet will later argue that because his ancestor was Edward's third son, he should be king rather than Henry of Lancaster, descended from Edward's fourth son. Mortimer then confirms Plantagenet's ambitions by bequeathing him the Mortimer family's claims to the crown. Taken together, these two scenes suggest that although the emotional basis of Plantagenet's cause is strong, its legal foundations are at least obscure. Unlike Talbot's battles on behalf of England, these quarrels and divisions at home are not resolved one way or the other, but left to fester and grow larger, ultimately threatening the nation's foreign wars.

By this method of juxtaposition, the play compares Talbot to Joan, to the English courtiers, and indirectly to the title character himself, the elusive Henry VI. The old soldiers at Henry's court – Bedford, Gloucester, Salisbury – share Talbot's principles but prove, like him, ineffectual politicians. Young John Talbot, steeped in his father's patriotic ideals, dies the same heroic but futile death as his father. Those who survive, including Winchester, York, Somerset, and Suffolk, are willing and even eager to sacrifice the public good for personal advancement. If the firmly rooted ethic of the Talbots cannot sustain them or their country in such circumstances, what can sustain the impressionable young king?

Certainly Henry will get no support from the scheming Suffolk or from Margaret of Anjou, the young French woman Suffolk loves. Typically, the play suggests the further darkening of Henry's environment by linking York's capture of Joan to Suffolk's of Margaret (V.5). These two women are led to very different fates: one must be burned alive, the other will be married to a king. Joan struggles to avoid her death, denying her peasant origins, then claiming both chastity and pregnancy as reasons she should live. Margaret, on the other hand, complies easily with Suffolk's wishes, agrees to marry Henry, and implicitly accepts an extramarital attachment as part of the bargain. Yet both women behave under compulsion, subject to the purposes of powerful men. Again, Shakespeare's method of juxtaposition sets up implied comparisons between the two pairs. The audience is invited to compare Joan with Margaret and to doubt the honesty of both. Similarly, Suffolk's tainted motives reflect on those of York. By turning his fury on Joan, York disguises his own responsibility for the English defeat in France. By advancing Margaret to the throne of England, Suffolk fashions her into a continuation by other means of the military threat once posed by Joan. Like the boy king himself, Joan and Margaret are pawns, treated not according to the standards of chivalry, but according to the needs and ambitions of the men who control them.

The dramatization of Henry's marriage to Margaret

does not end at the close of *1 Henry VI*, but continues until Henry's death in *3 Henry VI*. Shakespeare even extends Margaret's role past the end of *3 Henry VI* by having her appear, unhistorically, in *Richard III*. Because the plays in the Henry VI sequence, including *Richard III*, are closely related and seem to have been written at about the same time, they are known as Shakespeare's first "tetralogy," or four-play series. Although each of these plays is a full-length drama, the later ones continue several of the story lines begun earlier. Their action stretches from the funeral of Henry V in 1422 to the defeat of Richard III in 1485, but they may never have been staged as a continuous series until the twentieth century. Scholars have disagreed about the order in which Shakespeare wrote the plays, some arguing that *1 Henry VI* was drafted after *2 Henry VI* and *3 Henry VI* to provide an introduction. No matter how the Henry VI series was composed or first presented, however, the epilogue to Shakespeare's *Henry V* suggests the playwright's confidence that his audience knew all three plays and thought of them as a sequence:

Henry the Sixth, in infant bands crowned king
Of France and England, did this king succeed;
Whose state so many had the managing
That they lost France, and made his England bleed:
Which oft our stage hath shown.

(Epilogue, 9-13)

Some students of the plays have wondered whether Shakespeare wrote everything in the first tetralogy, a difficult question in the Tudor-Stuart period, when playwrights routinely collaborated and rewrote one another's work, much as screenwriters do today. Taken as a whole, however, the three Henry VI plays plus *Richard III* present a developing dramatic picture of England's political fortunes during the Wars of the Roses. (The plays of the second tetralogy, *Richard II, 1 Henry IV, 2 Henry IV,* and

Henry V, concern an earlier period, 1399–1420, and are not so closely connected as the first four.)

Shakespeare was one of the most important Elizabethan authors of English history plays. Some scholars even consider him the first dramatist to use English history to comment on his own era. Yet his works violate most modern ideas of how history should be written. These dramas mingle source material, what we might think of as fact, with material created by the author, or fiction. It seems clear, however, that Elizabethan scholars, writers, and audiences did not look at history the way we do. The chroniclers Hall and Holinshed, for example, gathered their narratives of medieval English history not from primary documents or eyewitness accounts, but from earlier chronicles and literary stories about the fall of princes. For the Tudors, the purpose of retelling the history of the period from Richard II to Richard III was not so much to achieve a scientific re-creation of events as to point out morals and cautionary tales. The example of a king such as Henry VI, later perceived as a failure, could help the Elizabethans avoid calamities like the Wars of the Roses. Whether the motives and actions attributed to Henry and his nobles were matters of fact or merely possible explanations seems to have mattered less than the need to avoid behaviors that might lead to similar disasters. Perhaps Henry V was in reality not the consummate warrior-politician that Shakespeare sketches at the start of *1 Henry VI,* and perhaps society did not really fail Henry VI in the ways shown in the plays. Nevertheless, an Elizabethan might have replied, it could have happened this way, and our era needs to understand and avoid such situations. As William Baldwin put it in *A Mirror for Magistrates* (1559), "where the ambitious seek no office, there no doubt offices are duly minist'red; and where offices are duly minist'red, it cannot be chosen but the people are good, whereof must needs follow a good commonweal. For if the officers be good, the people cannot be ill. Thus

the goodness or badness of any realm lieth in the goodness or badness of the rulers."

By most measures, the language of the Henry VI plays is
stately and formal. The editors of the Oxford Shakespeare
have devised what they call a "colloquialism-in-verse"
index, charting contractions and other abbreviated linguis-
tic forms, and find *1 Henry VI* to be the least colloquial of
all Shakespearean plays. Nobody in this work says anything
like Richard III's casual observation on the eve of battle,
". . . we must have knocks. Ha, must we not?" (V.3.5).
While much sixteenth-century language sounds ornate to
the modern ear, comparison of the Henry VI plays to the
body of Shakespeare's work shows that the dialogue of this
series observes the conventions of formal oratory more than
many of his other dramas. In *1 Henry VI,* Bedford's opening speech over the body of Henry V offers an example:

> Hung be the heavens with black! Yield, day, to night!
> Comets, importing change of times and states,
> Brandish your crystal tresses in the sky,
> And with them scourge the bad revolting stars
> That have consented unto Henry's death –
> King Henry the Fifth, too famous to live long.
> England ne'er lost a king of so much worth.
>
> (I.1.1–7)

Bedford's elaborate way of cursing fate for the death of his
king includes an invocation of the heavens and decorative
metaphors such as "crystal tresses" for comets' tails (which
then become whips to punish the "bad" stars). Of course,
Bedford tends to talk like this at other times, as when he
calls back the English troops after the recapture of Orléans:

> The day begins to break and night is fled,
> Whose pitchy mantle overveiled the earth.
> Here sound retreat and cease our hot pursuit.
>
> (II.2.1–3)

But many other speakers adopt the same high rhetorical style, making it the idiom of the play, and not just of particular characters. Joan la Pucelle, conjuring Burgundy to change sides, also uses elaborate and conventional similes:

> Look on thy country, look on fertile France,
> And see the cities and the towns defaced
> By wasting ruin of the cruel foe.
> As looks the mother on her lowly babe
> When death doth close his tender-dying eyes,
> See, see the pining malady of France;
> Behold the wounds, the most unnatural wounds,
> Which thou thyself hast given her woeful breast.
>   (III.7.44-51)

Since this persuasion works, at least on Burgundy, we cannot take it as an indication that Joan is an uninspired speaker. In fact, she and others can sometimes lift the oratorical style to something both plainer and more striking:

> Glory is like a circle in the water,
> Which never ceaseth to enlarge itself
> Till, by broad spreading, it disperse to nought.
> With Henry's death, the English circle ends.
> Dispersèd are the glories it included.
> Now am I like that proud insulting ship
> Which Caesar and his fortune bore at once.
>   (I.3.112-18)

There is very little prose in the Henry VI sequence, and almost none at all in *1 Henry VI*. Even when thoughts and words soar above the ordinary, the characters speak in balanced, largely end-stopped lines. This verse style suits the play's ceremonial tone as well as its structure, which displays action as a series of speaking pictures.

Perhaps surprisingly, the picture of Talbot dying with his dead son in his arms, formally enhanced by the rhymed couplets that dominate the scene, does not conclude the play. The last act encompasses the far less noble death of Joan, which nevertheless may evoke some pity for a peasant girl trapped and taunted by powerful men. It also brings forward the idea of a peace secured with a politically and economically advantageous marriage for Henry, then immediately undermines that possibility by introducing Margaret on the arm of the scheming Suffolk. Shakespeare's decision to continue the play past Talbot's end shows that he did not conceive of it as the tragedy of Talbot or of chivalric heroism. Instead, the play is a chapter in the long decline of England under Henry VI. In this first part, the audience sees the fading of the English empire in France. In the last act of *1 Henry VI,* the insubordination that contributed to England's defeat turns its treacherous face toward home.

In the intrigues of Winchester, York, Suffolk, and Margaret, we see danger to Gloucester and his ideals of honorable statecraft. As Margaret brings home the threat of heterogeneous influences previously represented by Joan, so Gloucester at court begins to look like Talbot on the battlefield, valiant but one-dimensional, dogged by dissension and conspiracy. Henry breaks his word to the Earl of Armagnac's daughter because he falls in love with Suffolk's description of Margaret. This is a clear indication that Henry's character has not only been neglected but also corrupted by the schemers around him. He behaves like Charles of France or even like Suffolk himself, linking his kingdom's fate to his own sexual whims. Lovesick, the young king retires to contemplate these new feelings: "I feel such sharp dissension in my breast, / Such fierce alarums both of hope and fear, / As I am sick with working of my thoughts" (V.7.84–86). As Gloucester believes, and as the audience is likely to think as well, this is only the beginning of King Henry's grief.

JANIS LULL
University of Alaska Fairbanks

The First Part of Henry the Sixth
GENEALOGICAL CHART

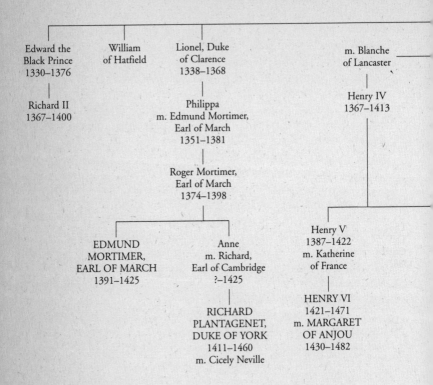

Edward the
Black Prince
1330–1376

William
of Hatfield

Lionel, Duke
of Clarence
1338–1368

m. Blanche
of Lancaster

Richard II
1367–1400

Philippa
m. Edmund Mortimer,
Earl of March
1351–1381

Henry IV
1367–1413

Roger Mortimer,
Earl of March
1374–1398

EDMUND
MORTIMER,
EARL OF MARCH
1391–1425

Anne
m. Richard,
Earl of Cambridge
?–1425

Henry V
1387–1422
m. Katherine
of France

RICHARD
PLANTAGENET,
DUKE OF YORK
1411–1460
m. Cicely Neville

HENRY VI
1421–1471
m. MARGARET
OF ANJOU
1430–1482

❧ Names of characters in the play appear in capitals.
Many persons not significant to *1 Henry VI* are omitted.

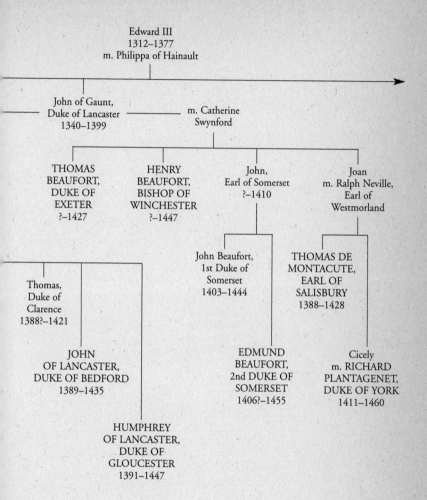

Edward III
1312–1377
m. Philippa of Hainault

John of Gaunt,
Duke of Lancaster ——————— m. Catherine
1340–1399   Swynford

THOMAS
BEAUFORT,
DUKE OF
EXETER
?–1427

HENRY
BEAUFORT,
BISHOP OF
WINCHESTER
?–1447

John,
Earl of Somerset
?–1410

Joan
m. Ralph Neville,
Earl of
Westmorland

Thomas,
Duke of
Clarence
1388?–1421

John Beaufort,
1st Duke of
Somerset
1403–1444

THOMAS DE
MONTACUTE,
EARL OF
SALISBURY
1388–1428

JOHN
OF LANCASTER,
DUKE OF BEDFORD
1389–1435

EDMUND
BEAUFORT,
2nd DUKE OF
SOMERSET
1406?–1455

Cicely
m. RICHARD
PLANTAGENET,
DUKE OF YORK
1411–1460

HUMPHREY
OF LANCASTER,
DUKE OF
GLOUCESTER
1391–1447

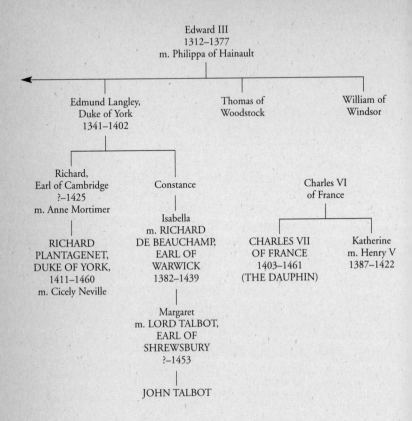

Edward III
1312–1377
m. Philippa of Hainault

Edmund Langley,
Duke of York
1341–1402

Thomas of
Woodstock

William of
Windsor

Richard,
Earl of Cambridge
?–1425
m. Anne Mortimer

Constance

Charles VI
of France

RICHARD
PLANTAGENET,
DUKE OF YORK,
1411–1460
m. Cicely Neville

Isabella
m. RICHARD
DE BEAUCHAMP,
EARL OF
WARWICK
1382–1439

CHARLES VII
OF FRANCE
1403–1461
(THE DAUPHIN)

Katherine
m. Henry V
1387–1422

Margaret
m. LORD TALBOT,
EARL OF
SHREWSBURY
?–1453

JOHN TALBOT

Note on the Text

THE PLAY WAS first printed in the folio collection of 1623 (the First Folio), as *The first Part of Henry the Sixt.* Gary Taylor has restated the traditional view that it is a collaborative work, probably written later than the other two plays that deal with the reign of Henry VI, and proposes that four authors were involved in the project – Shakespeare, Thomas Nashe, and two unidentified others. His arguments have not been refuted. The manuscript upon which the folio text is based appears to be the collaborative foul papers of the four authors involved.

This edition silently regularizes speech prefixes, expands stage directions where this appears necessary, and modernizes all spelling. Act and scene divisions, erratic in the folio, are here made on the basis of a stage cleared of all characters. All substantive emendations apart from these exceptions are recorded below. The adopted reading appears in italic type, followed by the folio reading in roman.

I.1 50 *marish* Nourish   60 *Rouen, Rheims,* Rheimes,   89 SECOND MESSEN-
GER Mess.   94 *René* Reynold   103 THIRD MESSENGER Mes.   157 *Fore Orléans* for Orleance is   176 *steal* send
I.3 9 *bred* breed   78 *five* fine
I.4 5 *knocketh* knocks   19 *My Lord* The Cardinall   29 *vizier* Vmpheir
36 *If* Ile canuas thee in thy broad Cardinalls Hat, / If   41 *purple* Scarlet
48 *I'll* I; *bishop's miter* Cardinalls Hat   55 *cloakèd* Scarlet   72 OFFICER
(not in F)   78 *Bishop* Cardinall   83 *bishop is* Cardinall's
I.5 8 *prince's spials* Princes espyals   10 *Wont* Went
I.6 5 *Duke* Earle   41 *Glasdale* Glansdale   44 *Lou* Lords   67 *Bear . . .
bury it.* (F places after I.6.64)   73 *like thee, Nero,* like thee,   79 *la Pucelle* de Puzel
I.7 3 *men* them   29 *style* Soyle
I.8 3 *la Pucelle* de Puzel   22 *of* or   29 *la Pucelle* de Puzel
II.1 5 SENTINEL Sent.   38 SENTINELS Sent.

II.2 20 *Arc* Acre

II.4 41 *from the tree are cropped* are cropt from the Tree   57 *law* you   132 *gentles* gentle

II.5 6–7 *Argue . . . Mortimer, / Nestor-like . . . care.* Nestor-like . . . Care, / Argue . . . Mortimer.   71 *King* (not in F)   75 *the third* third   76 *the king* hee   129 *mine ill* my will

III.1 52 GLOUCESTER Warw.   53 WARWICK (not in F, where this line and the prior three words, here assigned to Gloucester, are given to Warwick)   54 *so* see   167 *alone* all alone   203 *should lose* loose

IV.1 19 *Patay* Poictiers   48 *my* (not in F)   180 *I wist* I wish

IV.2 3 *captain* Captaines; *calls* call   15 FRENCH GENERAL Cap.   29 *fire* ryue

IV.3 17 LUCY 2. Mes.   30 LUCY Mes.   34 LUCY Mes.   47 LUCY Mes.

IV.4 16 *legions* Regions   19 *unadvantaged* in aduantage   26 *and* (not in F)   27 *René* Reignard   31 *horse* hoast

IV.5 39 *shamed* shame

IV.7 89 *have them* haue him   94 *with them* with him

V.1 59 *nor* neither

V.2 17–18 JOAN *Now . . . fear. / Of* Now . . . feare. / Pucel. Of

V.3 8 *speed and quick* speedy and quicke

V.4 15 *comest* comst

V.5 4–5 *And . . . side. / I . . . peace.* I . . . peace, / And . . . side   12 *his* her   18 *stream* streames   24 *here to hear* heere   92 *Assent* Consent   110 *countries* Country   135 *modestly* modestie

V.6 37 *one* me,   49 *Arc* Aire   68 *ingling* iugling   70 *we will* we'll

V.7 60 *That* (not in F)

The First Part of
Henry the Sixth

NAMES OF THE ACTORS

KING HENRY THE SIXTH, *Duke of Lancaster*

John of Lancaster, DUKE OF BEDFORD, *Regent of France,
    third son of King Henry the Fourth, the king's uncle*
Humphrey of Lancaster, DUKE OF GLOUCESTER, *the Lord
    Protector, fourth son of King Henry the Fourth,
    and the king's uncle*

Thomas Beaufort, DUKE OF EXETER, *brother of King
    Henry the Fourth, and the king's great-uncle*
Henry Beaufort, BISHOP (*later* CARDINAL) OF
    WINCHESTER, *Exeter's younger brother*
Edmund Beaufort, DUKE OF SOMERSET, *Exeter's nephew*

RICHARD PLANTAGENET, *son of Richard, late Earl of
    Cambridge, later* DUKE OF YORK *and Regent of France*

Richard de Beauchamp, EARL OF WARWICK
Thomas de Montacute, EARL OF SALISBURY
William de la Pole, EARL OF SUFFOLK
LORD TALBOT, *later Earl of Shrewsbury*
YOUNG JOHN TALBOT, *his son*
EDMUND MORTIMER, *Earl of March*
SIR WILLIAM GLASDALE
SIR THOMAS GARGRAVE
SIR JOHN FASTOLF
SIR WILLIAM LUCY
RICHARD WOODVILLE, *Lieutenant of the Tower of London*

MAYOR OF LONDON
VERNON
BASSET
A LAWYER *of the Temple*
A PAPAL LEGATE
KEEPERS, *or Jailers, to Mortimer*

CHARLES, *Dauphin of France*
RENÉ, *Duke of Anjou and titular King of Naples*
MARGARET, *his daughter*
DUKE OF ALENÇON
BASTARD OF ORLÉANS
DUKE OF BURGUNDY
GENERAL *of the French garrison at Bordeaux*
GOVERNOR OF PARIS
COUNTESS OF AUVERGNE
MASTER GUNNER *of Orléans*
A BOY, *his son*
JOAN *la Pucelle, also called Joan of Arc*
A SHEPHERD, *her father*
PORTER *of the Countess of Auvergne*
French SERGEANT
French SENTINEL
French SOLDIER
French SCOUT
FIENDS *appearing to Joan la Pucelle*

ATTENDANT LORDS, WARDER OF THE TOWER, ENGLISH
AND FRENCH HERALDS, SOLDIERS, COURTIERS,
MESSENGERS, SERVANTS

SCENE: *England and France*
*

The First Part of
Henry the Sixth

❧ **I.1** *Dead march. Enter the funeral of King Henry the*
Fifth, attended on by the Duke of Bedford, Humphrey
Duke of Gloucester, the Duke of Exeter, the Earl of
Warwick, the Bishop of Winchester, and the Duke of
Somerset.

BEDFORD
  Hung be the heavens with black! Yield, day, to night!
  Comets, importing change of times and states,   2
  Brandish your crystal tresses in the sky,
  And with them scourge the bad revolting stars   4
  That have consented unto Henry's death –
  King Henry the Fifth, too famous to live long.
  England ne'er lost a king of so much worth.
GLOUCESTER
  England ne'er had a king until his time.
  Virtue he had, deserving to command.   9
  His brandished sword did blind men with his beams.   10
  His arms spread wider than a dragon's wings.
  His sparkling eyes, replete with wrathful fire,
  More dazzled and drove back his enemies
  Than midday sun, fierce bent against their faces.
  What should I say? His deeds exceed all speech.

I.1 Westminster Abbey, London   **s.d.** *Dead* i.e., funeral   **2** *importing* fore-
telling   **4** *revolting* rebellious   **9** *Virtue* merit, power   **10** *his* its

16   He ne'er lift up his hand but conquerèd.

EXETER

17   We mourn in black; why mourn we not in blood?
      Henry is dead, and never shall revive.
      Upon a wooden coffin we attend,
20   And death's dishonorable victory
      We with our stately presence glorify,
22   Like captives bound to a triumphant car.
      What, shall we curse the planets of mishap,
      That plotted thus our glory's overthrow?
      Or shall we think the subtle-witted French
      Conjurers and sorcerers, that, afraid of him,
      By magic verses have contrived his end?

BISHOP OF WINCHESTER

      He was a king blest of the King of Kings.
      Unto the French, the dreadful judgment day
30   So dreadful will not be as was his sight.
      The battles of the Lord of Hosts he fought.
32   The church's prayers made him so prosperous.

GLOUCESTER

33   The church? Where is it? Had not churchmen prayed,
      His thread of life had not so soon decayed.
      None do you like but an effeminate prince,
      Whom like a schoolboy you may overawe.

BISHOP OF WINCHESTER

      Gloucester, whate'er we like, thou art Protector,
      And lookest to command the prince and realm.
39   Thy wife is proud: she holdeth thee in awe,
40   More than God or religious churchmen may.

GLOUCESTER

      Name not religion, for thou lov'st the flesh,
      And ne'er throughout the year to church thou go'st,

---

16 *lift* lifted; *but conquerèd* without conquering   **17** *in blood* by shedding blood   **22** *car* chariot   **32** *prosperous* successful   **33** *prayed* (with pun on "preyed")   **39** *Thy wife* Eleanor (guilty of ambition and witchcraft in *2 Henry VI*); *holdeth . . . awe* i.e., keeps you in subjection

Except it be to pray against thy foes.

BEDFORD
Cease, cease these jars, and rest your minds in peace.   44
Let's to the altar. Heralds, wait on us.

>   *Exeunt Warwick, Somerset,*
>   *and Heralds with coffin.*

Instead of gold, we'll offer up our arms –   46
Since arms avail not, now that Henry's dead.
Posterity, await for wretched years,   48
When, at their mothers' moistened eyes, babes shall
  suck,
Our isle be made a marish of salt tears,   50
And none but women left to wail the dead.
Henry the Fifth, thy ghost I invoke:
Prosper this realm; keep it from civil broils;   53
Combat with adverse planets in the heavens.
A far more glorious star thy soul will make
Than Julius Caesar or bright –

>   *Enter a Messenger.*

MESSENGER
My honorable lords, health to you all.
Sad tidings bring I to you out of France,
Of loss, of slaughter, and discomfiture.
Guyenne, Compiègne, Rouen, Rheims, Orléans,   60
Paris, Gisors, Poitiers are all quite lost.

BEDFORD
What sayst thou, man, before dead Henry's corpse?
Speak softly, or the loss of those great towns
Will make him burst his lead and rise from death.   64

GLOUCESTER   *To the Messenger*
Is Paris lost? Is Rouen yielded up?
If Henry were recalled to life again,

---

44 *jars* discords   46 *arms* weapons   48–50 *Posterity . . . tears* i.e., later gen-
erations, look for evil times, when mothers shall feed their children with
tears only   50 *marish* marsh   53 *broils* wars   64 *his lead* the lead lining of
his coffin

These news would cause him once more yield the
ghost.

EXETER   *To the Messenger*
How were they lost? What treachery was used?

MESSENGER
No treachery, but want of men and money.
70   Amongst the soldiers this is mutterèd:
That here you maintain several factions,
72   And whilst a field should be dispatched and fought,
73   You are disputing of your generals.
One would have ling'ring wars, with little cost;
75   Another would fly swift, but wanteth wings;
A third thinks, without expense at all,
By guileful fair words peace may be obtained.
Awake, awake, English nobility!
Let not sloth dim your honors new-begot.
80   Cropped are the flower-de-luces in your arms;
Of England's coat, one half is cut away.   *Exit.*

EXETER
82   Were our tears wanting to this funeral,
83   These tidings would call forth her flowing tides.

BEDFORD
Me they concern; Regent I am of France.
Give me my steelèd coat. I'll fight for France.
Away with these disgraceful wailing robes!
He removes his mourning robe.
87   Wounds will I lend the French, instead of eyes,
88   To weep their intermissive miseries.

---

72 *field* battle; *dispatched* settled 73 *of* about 75 *wanteth* lacks 80
Cropped plucked; *arms* coat of arms (Henry VI was supposed to be "heir of
France," since the French had yielded to his victorious father. Instead,
Charles the Dauphin was proclaimed king. Henry VI thus faced the loss of
his right to wear the fleur-de-lis, the national emblem of France, on his coat
of arms.) 82 *wanting* lacking 83 *her* England's 87 *Wounds . . . eyes* i.e.,
he will cause them to shed blood instead of tears 88 *intermissive* temporar-
ily interrupted, now to be resumed

Enter to them another Messenger, with letters.

SECOND MESSENGER
    Lords, view these letters, full of bad mischance.
    France is revolted from the English quite,   *90*
    Except some petty towns of no import.
    The Dauphin Charles is crownèd king in Rheims;
    The Bastard of Orléans with him is joined;
    René, Duke of Anjou, doth take his part;
    The Duke of Alençon flieth to his side.   *Exit.*

EXETER
    The dauphin crownèd king? All fly to him?
    O, whither shall *we* fly from this reproach?

GLOUCESTER
    We will not fly, but to our enemies' throats.
    Bedford, if thou be slack, I'll fight it out.

BEDFORD
    Gloucester, why doubt'st thou of my forwardness?   *100*
    An army have I mustered in my thoughts,
    Wherewith already France is overrun.
        Enter another Messenger.

THIRD MESSENGER
    My gracious lords, to add to your laments,
    Wherewith you now bedew King Henry's hearse,
    I must inform you of a dismal fight   *105*
    Betwixt the stout Lord Talbot and the French.   *106*

BISHOP OF WINCHESTER
    What, wherein Talbot overcame – is't so?

THIRD MESSENGER
    O no, wherein Lord Talbot was o'erthrown.
    The circumstance I'll tell you more at large.   *109*
    The tenth of August last, this dreadful lord,   *110*
    Retiring from the siege of Orléans,
    Having full scarce six thousand in his troop,   *112*

---

105 *dismal* unlucky   106 *stout* brave   109 *at large* in detail   110 *dreadful*
inspiring dread   112 *full scarce* i.e., scarcely full, barely

By three and twenty thousand of the French
Was round encompassèd and set upon.
No leisure had he to enrank his men.

116 He wanted pikes to set before his archers –
Instead whereof, sharp stakes plucked out of hedges
They pitchèd in the ground confusèdly,
To keep the horsemen off from breaking in.

120 More than three hours the fight continuèd,
Where valiant Talbot above human thought
Enacted wonders with his sword and lance.

123 Hundreds he sent to hell, and none durst stand him;
Here, there, and everywhere, enragèd he slew.
The French exclaimed the devil was in arms:

126 All the whole army stood agazed on him.
His soldiers, spying his undaunted spirit,

128 "A Talbot! A Talbot!" cried out amain,
And rushed into the bowels of the battle.

130 Here had the conquest fully been sealed up,

131 If Sir John Fastolf had not played the coward.

132 He, being in the vanguard placed behind,
With purpose to relieve and follow them,
Cowardly fled, not having struck one stroke.

135 Hence grew the general wrack and massacre.

136 Enclosèd were they with their enemies.

137 A base Walloon, to win the dauphin's grace,
Thrust Talbot with a spear into the back –
Whom all France, with their chief assembled strength,

140 Durst not presume to look once in the face.

---

116 *wanted pikes* lacked ironbound stakes (for defense against cavalry) **123**
stand face **126** *agazed on* astounded at **128** *A* to; *amain* vehemently **131**
Fastolf (as in the chronicles, but Shakespeare wrote "Falstaffe" in the folio;
not to be confused with the Falstaff of the Henry IV plays – this is Sir John
Fastolfe [c. 1378–1459], who rose to prominence under Henry V and then
the Duke of Bedford) **132** *being . . . behind* bringing up the rear of the vanguard **135** *wrack* destruction **136** *with* by **137** *Walloon* (citizen of a
province now in southern Belgium)

BEDFORD
  Is Talbot slain then? I will slay myself,
  For living idly here in pomp and ease
  Whilst such a worthy leader, wanting aid,
  Unto his dastard foemen is betrayed.

THIRD MESSENGER
  O no, he lives, but is took prisoner,
  And Lord Scales with him, and Lord Hungerford;
  Most of the rest slaughtered, or took likewise.

BEDFORD
  His ransom there is none but I shall pay.   148
  I'll hale the dauphin headlong from his throne;
  His crown shall be the ransom of my friend.   150
  Four of their lords I'll change for one of ours.   151
  Farewell, my masters; to my task will I.
  Bonfires in France forthwith I am to make,
  To keep our great Saint George's feast withal.   154
  Ten thousand soldiers with me I will take,
  Whose bloody deeds shall make all Europe quake.

THIRD MESSENGER
  So you had need. Fore Orléans, besieged,
  The English army is grown weak and faint.
  The Earl of Salisbury craveth supply,   159
  And hardly keeps his men from mutiny,   160
  Since they, so few, watch such a multitude.   *Exit.*

EXETER
  Remember, lords, your oaths to Henry sworn:
  Either to quell the dauphin utterly,
  Or bring him in obedience to your yoke.

BEDFORD
  I do remember it, and here take my leave
  To go about my preparation.   *Exit.*

---

148 *His . . . pay* i.e., my deeds of vengeance and rescue are all the ransom the
French can expect from us   151 *change* exchange (i.e., kill in retaliation –
since four Frenchmen are worth but one Englishman)   154 *Saint George's
feast* (traditionally April 23, but England's patron saint could be celebrated
with bonfires after any military victory)   159 *supply* reinforcements

GLOUCESTER

167   I'll to the Tower with all the haste I can,
      To view th' artillery and munition,
      And then I will proclaim young Henry king.   *Exit.*

EXETER

170   To Eltham will I, where the young king is,
      Being ordained his special governor,
      And for his safety there I'll best devise.   *Exit.*

BISHOP OF WINCHESTER

      Each hath his place and function to attend;
      I am left out; for me, nothing remains.
      But long I will not be Jack out of office.
      The king from Eltham I intend to steal,
177   And sit at chiefest stern of public weal.   *Exit.*

*

❧ **I.2** *Sound a flourish. Enter Charles the Dauphin,
the Duke of Alençon, and René Duke of Anjou,
marching with Drummer and Soldiers.*

CHARLES

1   Mars his true moving – even as in the heavens,
      So in the earth – to this day is not known.
3   Late did he shine upon the English side;
      Now we are victors: upon us he smiles.
5   What towns of any moment but we have?
      At pleasure here we lie near Orléans
7   Otherwhiles the famished English, like pale ghosts,
      Faintly besiege us one hour in a month.

---

167 *Tower* Tower of London   170 *Eltham* the royal residence, south of London   177 *at chiefest stern* as steersman, at the helm
   I.2 Near Orléans, France   **s.d.** *flourish* fanfare of trumpets   1 *Mars . . . moving* Mars's precise movement (the planet's seemingly eccentric orbit was a source of astronomical controversy)   3 *Late* lately   5 *of . . . have* i.e., of any importance that we do not possess   7 *Otherwhiles* while occasionally

ALENÇON
    They want their porridge and their fat bull beeves.   9
    Either they must be dieted like mules,   10
    And have their provender tied to their mouths,
    Or piteous they will look, like drownèd mice.
RENÉ
    Let's raise the siege. Why live we idly here?   13
    Talbot is taken, whom we wont to fear.   14
    Remaineth none but mad-brained Salisbury,
    And he may well in fretting spend his gall: 16
    Nor men nor money hath he to make war.   17
CHARLES
    Sound, sound, alarum! We will rush on them.   18
    Now for the honor of the forlorn French,
    Him I forgive my death that killeth me   20
    When he sees me go back one foot or flee.   *Exeunt.*

*

∾ **I.3** *Here alarum. The French are beaten back by the
English with great loss. Enter Charles the Dauphin,
the Duke of Alençon, and René Duke of Anjou.*

CHARLES
    Who ever saw the like? What men have I?
    Dogs, cowards, dastards! I would ne'er have fled,
    But that they left me 'midst my enemies.
RENÉ
    Salisbury is a desperate homicide.
    He fighteth as one weary of his life.
    The other lords, like lions wanting food,

---

9 *porridge* stew; *beeves* oxen, cattle **10** *dieted* fed **13** *raise* i.e., end by driving off the besieging armies **14** *wont* were accustomed **16** *spend his gall* expend his irritation **17** *Nor* neither **18** *alarum* call to arms
    I.3 Near Orléans

7   Do rush upon us as their hungry prey.

ALENÇON

8   Froissart, a countryman of ours, records
9   England all Olivers and Rolands bred
10   During the time Edward the Third did reign.
     More truly now may this be verified,
12   For none but Samsons and Goliases
     It sendeth forth to skirmish. One to ten?
14   Lean raw-boned rascals, who would e'er suppose
     They had such courage and audacity?

CHARLES

     Let's leave this town, for they are harebrained slaves,
17   And hunger will enforce them to be more eager.
     Of old I know them: rather with their teeth
     The walls they'll tear down, than forsake the siege.

RENÉ

20   I think by some odd gimmers or device
21   Their arms are set, like clocks, still to strike on,
     Else ne'er could they hold out so as they do.
     By my consent we'll even let them alone.

ALENÇON

     Be it so.
       Enter the Bastard of Orléans.

BASTARD

     Where's the Prince Dauphin? I have news for him.

CHARLES

     Bastard of Orléans, thrice welcome to us.

BASTARD

27   Methinks your looks are sad, your cheer appalled.
     Hath the late overthrow wrought this offense?
     Be not dismayed, for succor is at hand.

---

7 *hungry* arousing hunger   8 *Froissart* a fourteenth-century French chronicler   9 *England . . . bred* i.e., England's knights were all as chivalrous as the best who followed Charlemagne   12 *Goliases* Goliaths   14 *rascals* wretches   17 *eager* (1) fierce, (2) hungry   20 *gimmers* gimmals, mechanical joints for transmitting motion, as in clockwork   21 *still* continually   27 *cheer appalled* countenance made pale and downcast

A holy maid hither with me I bring,   30
Which, by a vision sent to her from heaven,
Ordainèd is to raise this tedious siege
And drive the English forth the bounds of France.
The spirit of deep prophecy she hath,
Exceeding the nine sibyls of old Rome.   35
What's past and what's to come she can descry.
Speak: shall I call her in? Believe my words,
For they are certain and unfallible.

CHARLES
Go call her in.   *Exit Bastard.*
            But first, to try her skill,
René stand thou as dauphin in my place.   40
Question her proudly; let thy looks be stern.
By this means shall we sound what skill she hath.   42
    Enter the Bastard of Orléans with Joan la Pucelle,
    armed.

RENÉ   *As Charles*
Fair maid, is't thou wilt do these wondrous feats?

JOAN
René, is't thou that thinkest to beguile me?
Where is the dauphin? *(To Charles)* Come, come from
  behind.
I know thee well, though never seen before.
Be not amazed. There's nothing hid from me.
In private will I talk with thee apart.
Stand back you lords, and give us leave awhile.
    René, Alençon, and Bastard stand apart.

RENÉ   *To Alençon and Bastard*
She takes upon her bravely, at first dash.   50

JOAN
Dauphin, I am by birth a shepherd's daughter,
My wit untrained in any kind of art.

---

35 *sibyls* prophetesses in the ancient world   42 *sound* test; **s.d.** *Pucelle* virgin
50 *takes . . . bravely* plays her part well

53   Heaven and our Lady gracious hath it pleased
        To shine on my contemptible estate.
        Lo, whilst I waited on my tender lambs,
        And to sun's parching heat displayed my cheeks,
        God's mother deignèd to appear to me,
        And in a vision, full of majesty,
        Willed me to leave my base vocation
60   And free my country from calamity.
        Her aid she promised, and assured success.
        In complete glory she revealed herself –
63   And whereas I was black and swart before,
64   With those clear rays which she infused on me
        That beauty am I blest with, which you may see.
        Ask me what question thou canst possible,
        And I will answer unpremeditated.
        My courage try by combat, if thou dar'st,
        And thou shalt find that I exceed my sex.
70   Resolve on this: thou shalt be fortunate,
71   If thou receive me for thy warlike mate.

CHARLES
72   Thou hast astonished me with thy high terms.
73   Only this proof I'll of thy valor make:
74   In single combat thou shalt buckle with me.
75   An if thou vanquishest, thy words are true;
76   Otherwise, I renounce all confidence.

JOAN
        I am prepared. Here is my keen-edged sword,
        Decked with five flower-de-luces on each side –
        The which at Touraine, in Saint Katherine's church-
          yard,
80   Out of a great deal of old iron I chose forth.

---

53 *our Lady gracious* the Virgin Mary   63 *swart* dark, swarthy   64 *With* by virtue of; *infused* shed   70 *Resolve on* be sure of   71 *warlike mate* (1) co-worker, (2) lover   72 *high terms* lofty language   73 *proof* trial   74 *buckle* (1) contend, (2) make love   75 *An if* if   76 *confidence* (1) firm trust, (2) intimacy

CHARLES
   Then come a God's name. I fear no woman.   81
JOAN
   And while I live, I'll ne'er fly from a man.
     Here they fight, and Joan la Pucelle overcomes.
CHARLES
   Stay, stay thy hands! Thou art an Amazon,
   And fightest with the sword of Deborah.   84
JOAN
   Christ's mother helps me, else I were too weak.
CHARLES
   Whoe'er helps thee, 'tis thou that must help me.
   Impatiently I burn with thy desire.   87
   My heart and hands thou hast at once subdued.
   Excellent Pucelle if thy name be so,
   Let me thy servant, and not sovereign, be.   90
   'Tis the French dauphin sueth to thee thus.
JOAN
   I must not yield to any rites of love,
   For my profession's sacred from above.
   When I have chasèd all thy foes from hence,
   Then will I think upon a recompense.
CHARLES
   Meantime, look gracious on thy prostrate thrall.
RENÉ   *To the other Lords apart*
   My lord, methinks, is very long in talk.
ALENÇON
   Doubtless he shrives this woman to her smock,   98
   Else ne'er could he so long protract his speech.
RENÉ
   Shall we disturb him, since he keeps no mean?   100

---

81 *a* in   84 *Deborah* Hebrew prophetess, judge over Israel, and successful commander of the army against Sisera (Judges 4)   87 *thy desire* desire for you   90 *servant* lover   98 *shrives* examines; *shrives . . . smock* (1) hears her confession completely, (2) examines her intimately (smock = undergarments)   100 *keeps no mean* is immoderate

ALENÇON

    He may mean more than we poor men do know.

    These women are shrewd tempters with their tongues.

RENÉ   *To Charles*

103   My lord, where are you? What devise you on?

    Shall we give o'er Orléans, or no?

JOAN

105   Why, no, I say. Distrustful recreants,

    Fight till the last gasp; I'll be your guard.

CHARLES

    What she says, I'll confirm. We'll fight it out.

JOAN

    Assigned am I to be the English scourge.

    This night the siege assurèdly I'll raise.

110   Expect Saint Martin's summer, halcyon's days,

    Since I have entered into these wars.

    Glory is like a circle in the water,

    Which never ceaseth to enlarge itself

    Till, by broad spreading, it disperse to nought.

    With Henry's death, the English circle ends.

    Dispersèd are the glories it included.

117   Now am I like that proud insulting ship

    Which Caesar and his fortune bore at once.

CHARLES

119   Was Muhammad inspirèd with a dove?

120   Thou with an eagle art inspirèd then.

121   Helen, the mother of great Constantine,

---

103 *devise* decide 105 *recreants* cowards 110 *Saint Martin's summer* i.e., Indian summer (since Saint Martin's Day is November 11; hence, success after a period of stormy fortune); *halcyon's days* a period of calm around December when the kingfisher – halcyon – supposedly breeds in a nest on the sea 117–18 *Now . . . once* (according to Plutarch, Caesar, aboard a small vessel in a storm, calmed the mariners with the thought that Caesar and his fortune were proof against drowning) 119 *Muhammad . . . dove* (Muhammad reputedly taught a dove to take feed at his ears; he claimed that the dove was the Holy Ghost and that it brought him divine revelation) 121 *Helen* Saint Helena, purported discoverer of the True Cross

Nor yet Saint Philip's daughters were like thee.   122
Bright star of Venus, fall'n down on the earth,
How may I reverently worship thee enough?
ALENÇON
Leave off delays, and let us raise the siege.
RENÉ
Woman, do what thou canst to save our honors.
Drive them from Orléans, and be immortalized.
CHARLES
Presently we'll try. Come, let's away about it.   128
No prophet will I trust, if she prove false.   *Exeunt.*

*

❧ **I.4** *Enter Humphrey Duke of Gloucester, with his
Servingmen in blue coats.*

GLOUCESTER
I am come to survey the Tower this day.   1
Since Henry's death, I fear there is conveyance.   2
Where be these warders, that they wait not here?   3
    A Servingman knocketh on the gates.
Open the gates: 'tis Gloucester that calls.
FIRST WARDER   *Within the Tower*
Who's there that knocketh so imperiously?
GLOUCESTER'S FIRST MAN
It is the noble Duke of Gloucester.
SECOND WARDER   *Within the Tower*
Whoe'er he be, you may not be let in.
GLOUCESTER'S FIRST MAN
Villains, answer you so the Lord Protector?   8

---

122 *Saint Philip's daughters* i.e., prophesying virgins (Acts 21:9) **128**
Presently immediately
  I.4 The Tower of London **s.d.** *blue coats* (customarily worn by servingmen)
1 *survey* inspect **2** *conveyance* sharp dealings, theft **3** *warders* guards **8**
Villains peasants, scoundrels

FIRST WARDER   *Within the Tower*
    The Lord protect him, so we answer him.
10   We do no otherwise than we are willed.
GLOUCESTER
    Who willèd you? Or whose will stands, but mine?
    There's none Protector of the realm but I.
      To Servingmen
13   Break up the gates. I'll be your warrantize.
    Shall I be flouted thus by dunghill grooms?
      Gloucester's Men rush at the Tower gates.
WOODVILLE   *Within the Tower*
    What noise is this? What traitors have we here?
GLOUCESTER
    Lieutenant, is it you whose voice I hear?
    Open the gates! Here's Gloucester, that would enter.
WOODVILLE   *Within the Tower*
    Have patience, noble duke: I may not open.
    My Lord of Winchester forbids.
20   From him I have express commandement
    That thou, nor none of thine, shall be let in.
GLOUCESTER
    Fainthearted Woodville! Prizest him 'fore me? –
    Arrogant Winchester, that haughty prelate,
24   Whom Henry, our late sovereign, ne'er could brook?
    Thou art no friend to God or to the king.
    Open the gates, or I'll shut thee out shortly.
SERVINGMEN
    Open the gates unto the Lord Protector,
28   Or we'll burst them open, if that you come not quickly.
      Enter, to the Lord Protector at the Tower gates, the
      Bishop of Winchester and his Men in tawny coats.
BISHOP OF WINCHESTER
    How now, ambitious vizier! What means this?

---

10 *willed* commanded   **13** *warrantize* authorization   **20** *commandement* (pronounced with four syllables)   **24** *brook* endure   **28 s.d.** *tawny coats* (worn by summoners of an ecclesiastical court)

GLOUCESTER

   Peeled priest, dost thou command me to be shut out?   30

BISHOP OF WINCHESTER

   I do, thou most usurping proditor,   31
   And not "Protector," of the king or realm.

GLOUCESTER

   Stand back, thou manifest conspirator.
   Thou that contrived'st to murder our dead lord,   34
   Thou that giv'st whores indulgences to sin,   35
   If thou proceed in this thy insolence –

BISHOP OF WINCHESTER

   Nay, stand thou back! I will not budge a foot.
   This be Damascus, be thou cursèd Cain,   38
   To slay thy brother Abel, if thou wilt.   39

GLOUCESTER

   I will not slay thee, but I'll drive thee back.   40
   Thy purple robes, as a child's bearing cloth,   41
   I'll use to carry thee out of this place.

BISHOP OF WINCHESTER

   Do what thou dar'st, I beard thee to thy face.   43

GLOUCESTER

   What, am I dared and bearded to my face?
   Draw, men, for all this privilegèd place.   45
     All draw their swords.
   Blue coats to tawny coats! – Priest, beware your beard.
   I mean to tug it, and to cuff you soundly.
   Under my feet I'll stamp thy bishop's miter.
   In spite of pope, or dignities of church,   49

---

30 *Peeled* shaven, tonsured   **31** *proditor* traitor   **34** *dead lord* i.e., Henry V
35 *giv'st . . . sin* (Bishop Beaufort historically received revenue from whore-
houses in the London suburb of Southwark)   **38** *Damascus* (popular belief
held that Cain slew Abel on the site of this later city)   **39** *brother* (Bishop
Beaufort is actually Gloucester's half uncle)   **41** *bearing cloth* christening
robe   **43** *beard* defy   **45** *for . . . place* i.e., despite ordinances forbidding
drawing of weapons near a royal residence   **49** *dignities* dignitaries

50   Here by the cheeks I'll drag thee up and down.

BISHOP OF WINCHESTER

51   Gloucester, thou wilt answer this before the pope.

GLOUCESTER

52   Winchester goose! I cry, "A rope, a rope!"
     To his Servingmen
   Now beat them hence. Why do you let them stay?
     To Winchester
   Thee I'll chase hence, thou wolf in sheep's array.
   Out, tawny coats! Out, cloakèd hypocrite!
     Here Gloucester's Men beat out the Bishop's Men.
     Enter in the hurly-burly the Mayor of London
     and his Officers.

MAYOR

   Fie, lords! – that you, being supreme magistrates,

57   Thus contumeliously should break the peace.

GLOUCESTER

   Peace, mayor, thou know'st little of my wrongs.
   Here's Beaufort – that regards nor God nor king –

60   Hath here distrained the Tower to his use.

BISHOP OF WINCHESTER   *To Mayor*

   Here's Gloucester – a foe to citizens,

62   One that still motions war, and never peace,
   O'ercharging your free purses with large fines –
   That seeks to overthrow religion,
   Because he is Protector of the realm,
   And would have armor here out of the Tower

67   To crown himself king and suppress the prince.

GLOUCESTER

   I will not answer thee with words but blows.
     Here the factions skirmish again.

MAYOR

69   Nought rests for me, in this tumultuous strife,

---

51 *answer* pay for   **52** *Winchester goose* a venereal disorder   **57** *contume-liously* contemptuously   **60** *distrained* confiscated   **62** *still motions* always advocates   **67** *prince* king (i.e., Henry VI)   **69** *rests* is left

But to make open proclamation.   70
Come, officer, as loud as e'er thou canst, cry.

OFFICER   All manner of men, assembled here in arms
this day against God's peace and the king's, we charge
and command you in his highness' name to repair to
your several dwelling places, and not to wear, handle,
or use any sword, weapon, or dagger henceforward,
upon pain of death.
        The skirmishes cease.

GLOUCESTER
Bishop, I'll be no breaker of the law.
But we shall meet and break our minds at large.   79

BISHOP OF WINCHESTER
Gloucester, we'll meet to thy cost, be sure.   80
Thy heartblood I will have for this day's work.

MAYOR
I'll call for clubs, if you will not away.   82
        Aside
This bishop is more haughty than the devil.

GLOUCESTER
Mayor, farewell. Thou dost but what thou mayst.

BISHOP OF WINCHESTER
Abominable Gloucester, guard thy head,
For I intend to have it ere long.   86
                        Exeunt both factions severally.

MAYOR   *To Officers*
See the coast cleared, and then we will depart. –
Good God, these nobles should such stomachs bear!   88
I myself fight not once in forty year.   *Exeunt.*

                        *

---

79 *break our minds* (1) express our views, (2) crack heads; *at large* at length
82 *call for clubs* (rallying cry for London apprentices with their clubs)   86
s.d. *severally* separately   88 *stomachs* tempers

❧ **I.5** *Enter the Master Gunner of Orléans with his Boy.*

MASTER GUNNER

1   Sirrah, thou know'st how Orléans is besieged,
    And how the English have the suburbs won.

BOY
    Father, I know, and oft have shot at them;
4   Howe'er, unfortunate, I missed my aim.

MASTER GUNNER
    But now thou shalt not. Be thou ruled by me.
    Chief Master Gunner am I of this town;
7   Something I must do to procure me grace.
8   The prince's spials have informèd me
    How the English, in the suburbs close entrenched,
10   Wont, through a secret grate of iron bars
    In yonder tower, to overpeer the city,
    And thence discover how with most advantage
    They may vex us with shot or with assault.
14   To intercept this inconvenience,
15   A piece of ordnance 'gainst it I have placed,
    And even these three days have I watched, if I could see
      them.
    Now do thou watch, for I can stay no longer.
    If thou spy'st any, run and bring me word,
    And thou shalt find me at the governor's.

BOY
20   Father, I warrant you, take you no care –
                  Exit Master Gunner at one door.
    I'll never trouble you, if I may spy them.
                      Exit at the other door.

*

I.5 Orléans   1 *Sirrah* (form of address to social inferiors)   4 *Howe'er* although   7 *grace* honor   8 *spials* spies   10 *Wont* are accustomed   14 *inconvenience* mischief   15 *piece of ordnance* artillery; *'gainst* directed toward

∾ **I.6** *Enter the Earl of Salisbury and Lord Talbot above
on the turrets with others, among them Sir Thomas
Gargrave and Sir William Glasdale.*

SALISBURY
    Talbot, my life, my joy, again returned?
    How wert thou handled, being prisoner?
    Or by what means got'st thou to be released?
    Discourse, I prithee, on this turret's top.

TALBOT
    The Duke of Bedford had a prisoner,
    Called the brave Lord Ponton de Santrailles;
    For him was I exchanged and ransomèd.
    But with a baser man-of-arms by far   8
    Once in contempt they would have bartered me –
    Which I, disdaining, scorned, and cravèd death   *10*
    Rather than I would be so pilled esteemed.   11
    In fine, redeemed I was, as I desired.   12
    But O, the treacherous Fastolf wounds my heart,
    Whom with my bare fists I would execute
    If I now had him brought into my power.

SALISBURY
    Yet tell'st thou not how thou wert entertained.   16

TALBOT
    With scoffs and scorns and contumelious taunts.
    In open marketplace produced they me,
    To be a public spectacle to all.
    "Here," said they, "is the terror of the French,   *20*
    The scarecrow that affrights our children so."
    Then broke I from the officers that led me
    And with my nails digged stones out of the ground

I.6 Tower before the walls of Orléans **s.d.** *turrets* i.e., rear-stage gallery or
some higher point in the theater **8** *baser man-of-arms* soldier of lower birth
or rank **11** *pilled* peeled (i.e., stripped of dignity) **12** *In fine* in short; *re-
deemed* ransomed **16** *entertained* treated

To hurl at the beholders of my shame.
My grisly countenance made others fly.
None durst come near, for fear of sudden death.
In iron walls they deemed me not secure:
So great fear of my name 'mongst them were spread
That they supposed I could rend bars of steel
30 And spurn in pieces posts of adamant.
31 Wherefore a guard of chosen shot I had
32 That walked about me every minute while;
And if I did but stir out of my bed,
34 Ready they were to shoot me to the heart.
  The Boy passes over the stage with a linstock.

SALISBURY
I grieve to hear what torments you endured.
But we will be revenged sufficiently.
Now it is suppertime in Orléans.
Here, through this grate, I count each one,
And view the Frenchmen how they fortify.
40 Let us look in: the sight will much delight thee. –
Sir Thomas Gargrave and Sir William Glasdale,
42 Let me have your express opinions
43 Where is best place to make our batt'ry next.
  They look through the grate.

GARGRAVE
44 I think at the north gate, for there stands Lou.

GLASDALE
45 And I here, at the bulwark of the bridge.

TALBOT
46 For aught I see, this city must be famished
47 Or with light skirmishes enfeeblèd.
  Here they shoot off chambers within, and Salisbury
  and Gargrave fall down.

---

30 *spurn* kick 31 *chosen shot* outstanding marksmen 32 *every minute while*
every minute's space, constantly 34 **s.d.** *linstock* forked stick holding gunner's match 42 *express* definite 43 *batt'ry* artillery platform 44 *Lou* the
fortress of Saint Lou 45 *bulwark* fortification 46 *must be* will have to be
47 **s.d.** *they* i.e., the French

SALISBURY

  O Lord have mercy on us, wretched sinners!

GARGRAVE

  O Lord have mercy on me, woeful man!

TALBOT

  What chance is this that suddenly hath crossed us?   50
  Speak, Salisbury – at least, if thou canst, speak.
  How far'st thou, mirror of all martial men?   52
  One of thy eyes and thy cheek's side struck off?
  Accursèd tower! Accursèd fatal hand
  That hath contrived this woeful tragedy!
  In thirteen battles Salisbury o'ercame;
  Henry the Fifth he first trained to the wars;
  Whilst any trump did sound or drum struck up
  His sword did ne'er leave striking in the field.   59
  Yet liv'st thou, Salisbury? Though thy speech doth fail,   60
  One eye thou hast to look to heaven for grace.
  The sun with one eye vieweth all the world.
  Heaven, be thou gracious to none alive
  If Salisbury wants mercy at thy hands. –   64
  Sir Thomas Gargrave, hast thou any life?
  Speak unto Talbot. Nay, look up to him. –
  Bear hence his body; I will help to bury it.

                        Exit one with Gargrave's body.

  Salisbury, cheer thy spirit with this comfort:
  Thou shalt not die whiles –   69
  He beckons with his hand, and smiles on me,   70
  As who should say, "When I am dead and gone,
  Remember to avenge me on the French."
  Plantagenet, I will – and like thee, Nero,   73
  Play on the lute, beholding the towns burn.
  Wretched shall France be only in my name.   75

---

50 *chance* mischance 52 *mirror* best example 59 *leave* cease from 64
wants lacks 69 *whiles* until 73 *Plantagenet* (Salisbury is likened to Nero as
a type of heartless destroyer of cities; Talbot vows to emulate them both) 75
only in at the mere sound of

Here an alarum, and it thunders and lightens.
What stir is this? What tumult's in the heavens?
Whence cometh this alarum and the noise?
          Enter a Messenger.

MESSENGER

78   My lord, my lord, the French have gathered head.
      The dauphin, with one Joan la Pucelle joined,
80   A holy prophetess new risen up,
81   Is come with a great power to raise the siege.
              Here Salisbury lifteth himself up and groans.

TALBOT

      Hear, hear, how dying Salisbury doth groan!
      It irks his heart he cannot be revenged.
      Frenchmen, I'll be a Salisbury to you.
85   *Pucelle* or pucelle, dauphin or dogfish,
      Your hearts I'll stamp out with my horse's heels
      And make a quagmire of your mingled brains. –
88   Convey me Salisbury into his tent,
      And then we'll try what these dastard Frenchmen dare.
                  Alarum. Exeunt carrying Salisbury.

                         *

❧ **I.7** *Here an alarum again, and Lord Talbot pursueth
the Dauphin and driveth him. Then enter Joan la
Pucelle driving Englishmen before her and exeunt.
Then enter Lord Talbot.*

TALBOT

      Where is my strength, my valor, and my force?
      Our English troops retire; I cannot stay them.

---

78 gathered head assembled an army   **81** *power* army   **85** *Pucelle . . . pucelle*
(Talbot puns on the fact that *pucelle,* the French word for "virgin," sounds like
the English word [no longer in use] for "slut" and "young shad" [a kind of
fish]); *dauphin* (near homonym for "dolphin," believed to be the highest in the
chain of being among fish); *dogfish* a small shark (contemptibly low form of
fish)   **88** *me* for me
      I.7 In and before Orléans

A woman clad in armor chaseth men.
   Enter Joan la Pucelle.
Here, here she comes. *(To Joan)* I'll have a bout with   4
  thee.
Devil or devil's dam, I'll conjure thee.   5
Blood will I draw on thee – thou art a witch –   6
And straightway give thy soul to him thou serv'st.   7

JOAN
Come, come, 'tis only I that must disgrace thee.
   Here they fight.

TALBOT
Heavens, can you suffer hell so to prevail?
My breast I'll burst with straining of my courage   10
And from my shoulders crack my arms asunder
But I will chastise this high-minded strumpet.   12
   They fight again.

JOAN
Talbot, farewell. Thy hour is not yet come.
I must go victual Orléans forthwith.   14
   A short alarum, then the French pass over the stage
   and enter the town with Soldiers.
O'ertake me if thou canst. I scorn thy strength.
Go, go, cheer up thy hungry-starvèd men.
Help Salisbury to make his testament.
This day is ours, as many more shall be.
                   Exit into the town.

TALBOT
My thoughts are whirlèd like a potter's wheel.
I know not where I am nor what I do.   20

---

4 *bout* (1) fight, (2) sexual encounter   5 *conjure* constrain by sacred oath (a supernatural good, similar in method but opposite in intent to her supernatural evil)   6 *Blood . . . witch* (Talbot again proposes to fight black magic by virtuous magic, gaining power over her by obtaining a sample of her blood in honest combat)   7 *him* i.e., the devil   10 *courage* vital energy   12 *But I* if I do not; *high-minded* presumptuous   14 *victual* supply with provisions

21 A witch by fear, not force, like Hannibal
22 Drives back our troops and conquers as she lists.
23 So bees with smoke and doves with noisome stench
Are from their hives and houses driven away.
They called us, for our fierceness, English dogs;
Now, like to whelps, we crying run away.
    A short alarum. Enter English Soldiers.
Hark, countrymen: either renew the fight
28 Or tear the lions out of England's coat.
29 Renounce your style; give sheep in lions' stead.
30 Sheep run not half so treacherous from the wolf,
Or horse or oxen from the leopard,
As you fly from your oft-subduèd slaves.
    Alarum. Here another skirmish.
It will not be. Retire into your trenches.
You all consented unto Salisbury's death,
35 For none would strike a stroke in his revenge.
Pucelle is entered into Orléans
In spite of us or aught that we could do.
                                    Exeunt Soldiers.
O would I were to die with Salisbury!
The shame hereof will make me hide my head.
                            Exit. Alarum. Retreat.

                    *

---

21 *Hannibal* a Carthaginian general (who once rescued his army from encirclement by tying firebrands to the horns of 2,000 oxen and driving the oxen into the terrified Roman ranks)   22 *lists* pleases   23 *noisome* noxious   28 *coat* coat of arms (the English coat of arms displayed three recumbent lions)   29 *style* distinguishing mark; *give . . . stead* i.e., display sheep on your coat of arms as symbols of cowardice   30 *treacherous* cowardly and treasonous   35 *his revenge* in revenge of his death

ॐ **I.8** *Flourish. Enter on the walls Joan la Pucelle,*
Charles the Dauphin, René Duke of Anjou, the Duke
of Alençon, and French Soldiers with colors.

JOAN
  Advance our waving colors on the walls;   1
  Rescued is Orléans from the English.
  Thus Joan la Pucelle hath performed her word.
CHARLES
  Divinest creature, Astraea's daughter,   4
  How shall I honor thee for this success?
  Thy promises are like Adonis' garden,   6
  That one day bloomed and fruitful were the next.
  France, triumph in thy glorious prophetess!
  Recovered is the town of Orléans.
  More blessèd hap did ne'er befall our state.   10
RENÉ
  Why ring not out the bells aloud throughout the town?
  Dauphin, command the citizens make bonfires
  And feast and banquet in the open streets
  To celebrate the joy that God hath given us.
ALENÇON
  All France will be replete with mirth and joy
  When they shall hear how we have played the men.   16
CHARLES
  'Tis Joan, not we, by whom the day is won —
  For which I will divide my crown with her,
  And all the priests and friars in my realm
  Shall in procession sing her endless praise.   20
  A statelier pyramid to her I'll rear

I.8 In and before Orléans **s.d.** *on the walls* (in scenes I.5 through II.2 the
tiring-house gallery represents the defended walls of Orléans) **1** *Advance*
raise aloft **4** *Astraea* a goddess of justice, who lived among men during the
golden age but was forced to reascend to the heavens in the Iron Age; her return to earth would signal a new age of justice **6** *Adonis' garden* mythical
garden of eternal profusion **10** *hap* event **16** *played the* acted like

22   Than Rhodope's of Memphis ever was.
           In memory of her, when she is dead,
           Her ashes, in an urn more precious
25   Than the rich-jeweled coffer of Darius,
           Transported shall be at high festivals
           Before the kings and queens of France.
28   No longer on Saint Denis will we cry,
           But Joan la Pucelle shall be France's saint.
30   Come in, and let us banquet royally
           After this golden day of victory.   *Flourish. Exeunt.*

                                  *

∾ **II.1** *Enter on the walls a French Sergeant of a band,*
    with two Sentinels.

SERGEANT
           Sirs, take your places and be vigilant.
           If any noise or soldier you perceive
3   Near to the walls, by some apparent sign
4   Let us have knowledge at the court of guard.
SENTINEL
5   Sergeant, you shall.   *Exit Sergeant.*
                           Thus are poor servitors,
           When others sleep upon their quiet beds,
           Constrained to watch in darkness, rain, and cold.
           Enter Lord Talbot, the Dukes of Bedford and
           Burgundy, and Soldiers with scaling ladders, their
           drums beating a dead march.

---

22 *Rhodope* a Greek courtesan who became queen of Memphis and reputedly
built the Third Pyramid   **25** *coffer of Darius* (Alexander, vanquishing Darius
in battle, took from him a priceless jeweled chest, and was said to have
placed within it his most valued possession, the works of Homer)   **28** *Saint
Denis* the patron saint of France
    II.1 In and before Orléans   **3** *apparent* plain   **4** *court of guard* guardhouse
5 *servitors* common soldiers

TALBOT

    Lord Regent, and redoubted Burgundy –　　　　　　8
    By whose approach the regions of Artois,
    Wallon, and Picardy are friends to us –　　　　　10
    This happy night the Frenchmen are secure,　　11
    Having all day caroused and banqueted.
    Embrace we then this opportunity,
    As fitting best to quittance their deceit,　　　14
    Contrived by art and baleful sorcery.　　　　　15

BEDFORD

    Coward of France! How much he wrongs his fame,　16
    Despairing of his own arms' fortitude,
    To join with witches and the help of hell.

BURGUNDY

    Traitors have never other company.
    But what's that "Pucelle" whom they term so pure?　20

TALBOT

    A maid, they say.

BEDFORD　　　　　　A maid? And be so martial?

BURGUNDY

    Pray God she prove not masculine ere long.　　22
    If underneath the standard of the French　　　23
    She carry armor as she hath begun –　　　　　　24

TALBOT

    Well, let them practice and converse with spirits.　25
    God is our fortress, in whose conquering name
    Let us resolve to scale their flinty bulwarks.

---

8 *redoubted* distinguished   8–10 *Burgundy . . . us* (Burgundy's alliance with the English in the time of Henry V had brought support not only from the important Duchy of Burgundy, southeast of Paris, but from territories friendly to him in the Low Countries)   11 *secure* unsuspecting, overconfident   14 *quittance* repay   15 *art* black magic   16 *Coward* i.e., the dauphin; *fame* reputation   22 *prove not masculine* (1) turns out to be a man, (2) turns out to be carrying a male child   23 *standard of the French* (1) French ensign, (2) French penis   24 *carry armor* (1) wears armor, (2) bears the weight of an armed man (in intercourse)   25 *practice and converse* (1) scheme and talk, (2) have sex and be intimate

BEDFORD
  Ascend, brave Talbot. We will follow thee.

TALBOT
  Not all together. Better far, I guess,
30 That we do make our entrance several ways –
  That, if it chance the one of us do fail,
  The other yet may rise against their force.

BEDFORD
  Agreed. I'll to yon corner.

BURGUNDY   And I to this.

*Exeunt severally Bedford
and Burgundy with some Soldiers.*

TALBOT
  And here will Talbot mount, or make his grave.
  Now, Salisbury, for thee, and for the right
  Of English Henry, shall this night appear
  How much in duty I am bound to both.
  Talbot and his Soldiers scale the walls.

SENTINELS
  Arm! Arm! The enemy doth make assault!

ENGLISH SOLDIERS
39 Saint George! A Talbot!   *Exeunt above.*
  *Alarum. The French Soldiers leap o'er the walls in
  their shirts and exeunt. Enter several ways the Bastard
  of Orléans, the Duke of Alençon, and René Duke of
  Anjou, half ready and half unready.*

ALENÇON
40 How now, my lords? What, all unready so?

BASTARD
  Unready? Ay, and glad we scaped so well.

RENÉ
42 'Twas time, I trow, to wake and leave our beds,
  Hearing alarums at our chamber doors.

----

39 s.d. *o'er the walls* (some of the routed French, emerging from the tiring-house, leap from the rear-stage gallery down to the main stage; some use other entrances)   **42** *trow* believe

ALENÇON
    Of all exploits since first I followed arms
    Ne'er heard I of a warlike enterprise
    More venturous or desperate than this.

BASTARD
    I think this Talbot be a fiend of hell.

RENÉ
    If not of hell, the heavens sure favor him.

ALENÇON
    Here cometh Charles. I marvel how he sped.   49
      Enter Charles the Dauphin and Joan la Pucelle.

BASTARD
    Tut, holy Joan was his defensive guard.   50

CHARLES   *To Joan*
    Is this thy cunning, thou deceitful dame?   51
    Didst thou at first, to flatter us withal,   52
    Make us partakers of a little gain
    That now our loss might be ten times so much?

JOAN
    Wherefore is Charles impatient with his friend?
    At all times will you have my power alike?
    Sleeping or waking must I still prevail,
    Or will you blame and lay the fault on me? –
    Improvident soldiers, had your watch been good,   59
    This sudden mischief never could have fall'n.   60

CHARLES
    Duke of Alençon, this was your default,
    That, being captain of the watch tonight,   62
    Did look no better to that weighty charge.

ALENÇON
    Had all your quarters been as safely kept   64
    As that whereof I had the government,
    We had not been thus shamefully surprised.

---

49 *sped* fared 51 *cunning* skill, especially in sorcery 52 *flatter* encourage
with false hopes 59 *Improvident* negligent 60 *mischief* calamity 62
tonight last night 64 *kept* guarded

BASTARD
Mine was secure.

RENÉ   And so was mine, my lord.

CHARLES
And for myself, most part of all this night

69   Within her quarter and mine own precinct

70   I was employed in passing to and fro
About relieving of the sentinels.
Then how or which way should they first break in?

JOAN
Question, my lords, no further of the case,
How or which way. 'Tis sure they found some place

75   But weakly guarded, where the breach was made.

76   And now there rests no other shift but this –
To gather our soldiers, scattered and dispersed,

78   And lay new platforms to endamage them.
    Alarum. Enter an English Soldier.

ENGLISH SOLDIER   A Talbot! A Talbot!
    The French fly, leaving their clothes behind.

80   I'll be so bold to take what they have left.
The cry of "Talbot" serves me for a sword,
For I have loaden me with many spoils,
Using no other weapon but his name.   *Exit with spoils.*

*

∾ **II.2** *Enter Lord Talbot, the Dukes of Bedford and
Burgundy, a Captain, and Soldiers.*

BEDFORD
The day begins to break and night is fled,
Whose pitchy mantle overveiled the earth.
Here sound retreat and cease our hot pursuit.
    Retreat is sounded.

---

69 *her* i.e., Joan's   **75** *But* only   **76** *rests* remains; *shift* device   **78** *platforms*
schemes
   II.2 Within Orléans

TALBOT

Bring forth the body of old Salisbury
And here advance it in the marketplace,   5
The middle center of this cursèd town.   6

Exit one or more.

Now have I paid my vow unto his soul:
For every drop of blood was drawn from him   8
There hath at least five Frenchmen died tonight.
And that hereafter ages may behold   10
What ruin happened in revenge of him,
Within their chiefest temple I'll erect
A tomb, wherein his corpse shall be interred –
Upon the which, that every one may read,
Shall be engraved the sack of Orléans,
The treacherous manner of his mournful death,   16
And what a terror he had been to France.
But, lords, in all our bloody massacre
I muse we met not with the dauphin's grace,   19
His new-come champion, virtuous Joan of Arc,   20
Nor any of his false confederates.

BEDFORD

'Tis thought, Lord Talbot, when the fight began,
Roused on the sudden from their drowsy beds,
They did amongst the troops of armèd men
Leap o'er the walls for refuge in the field.

BURGUNDY

Myself, as far as I could well discern
For smoke and dusky vapors of the night,
Am sure I scared the dauphin and his trull,   28
When arm in arm they both came swiftly running,
Like to a pair of loving turtledoves   30
That could not live asunder day or night.
After that things are set in order here,

---

5 *advance* raise aloft (on a bier)   6 *middle . . . town* (the stage is now the center of Orléans)   8 *was* that was   16 *mournful* causing sorrow   19 *muse* wonder   20 *virtuous* (ironic)   28 *trull* whore

We'll follow them with all the power we have.
   Enter a Messenger.

MESSENGER
All hail, my lords! Which of this princely train
Call ye the warlike Talbot, for his acts
So much applauded through the realm of France?

TALBOT
Here is the Talbot. Who would speak with him?

MESSENGER
The virtuous lady, Countess of Auvergne,
With modesty admiring thy renown,
40   By me entreats, great lord, thou wouldst vouchsafe
41   To visit her poor castle where she lies,
That she may boast she hath beheld the man
43   Whose glory fills the world with loud report.

BURGUNDY
Is it even so? Nay, then I see our wars
Will turn unto a peaceful comic sport,
46   When ladies crave to be encountered with.
47   You may not, my lord, despise her gentle suit.

TALBOT
Ne'er trust me then, for when a world of men
Could not prevail with all their oratory,
50   Yet hath a woman's kindness overruled. –
And therefore tell her I return great thanks,
And in submission will attend on her. –
Will not your honors bear me company?

BEDFORD
54   No, truly, 'tis more than manners will.
And I have heard it said, "Unbidden guests
Are often welcomest when they are gone."

TALBOT
Well then, alone – since there's no remedy –
58   I mean to prove this lady's courtesy.

---

41 *lies* dwells   43 *report* (1) acclaim, (2) noise   46 *encountered with* (1) met,
(2) wooed   47 *gentle suit* well-bred request   54 *will* require   58 *prove* test

Come hither, captain.   59
 Talbot whispers something to the Captain.
      You perceive my mind?
CAPTAIN
 I do, my lord, and mean accordingly. *Exeunt severally.* 60
        ✳

∾ **II.3** *Enter the Countess of Auvergne and her Porter.*

COUNTESS
 Porter, remember what I gave in charge,   1
 And when you have done so, bring the keys to me.
PORTER
 Madam, I will.   *Exit.*
COUNTESS
 The plot is laid. If all things fall out right,
 I shall as famous be by this exploit
 As Scythian Tomyris by Cyrus' death.   6
 Great is the rumor of this dreadful knight,   7
 And his achievements of no less account.
 Fain would mine eyes be witness with mine ears,   9
 To give their censure of these rare reports.   10
  Enter Messenger and Lord Talbot.
MESSENGER
 Madam, according as your ladyship desired,
 By message craved, so is Lord Talbot come.
COUNTESS
 And he is welcome. What, is this the man?
MESSENGER
 Madam, it is.

---

59 *mind* intent **60** *mean* intend to act

II.3 The countess's castle, Auvergne **1** *gave in charge* ordered **6** *Tomyris*
queen of Scythia who overcame Cyrus in battle, and in revenge for her sons'
death had Cyrus's head thrown into a wineskin of human blood **7** *rumor*
reputation; *dreadful* dread-inspiring **9** *Fain* gladly **10** *censure* judgment;
rare remarkable

COUNTESS   Is this the scourge of France?

15   Is this the Talbot, so much feared abroad

16   That with his name the mothers still their babes?

     I see report is fabulous and false.

18   I thought I should have seen some Hercules,

19   A second Hector, for his grim aspect

20   And large proportion of his strong-knit limbs.

21   Alas, this is a child, a seely dwarf.

22   It cannot be this weak and writhled shrimp

     Should strike such terror to his enemies.

TALBOT

     Madam, I have been bold to trouble you.

     But since your ladyship is not at leisure,

     I'll sort some other time to visit you.

       He is going.

COUNTESS   *To Messenger*

     What means he now? Go ask him whither he goes.

MESSENGER

     Stay, my Lord Talbot, for my lady craves

     To know the cause of your abrupt departure.

TALBOT

30   Marry, for that she's in a wrong belief,

31   I go to certify her Talbot's here.

       Enter Porter with keys.

COUNTESS

     If thou be he, then art thou prisoner.

TALBOT

     Prisoner? To whom?

COUNTESS   To me, bloodthirsty lord;

34   And for that cause I trained thee to my house.

35   Long time thy shadow hath been thrall to me,

     For in my gallery thy picture hangs;

---

15 *abroad* everywhere   16 *still* quiet   18, 19 *Hercules, Hector* (types of manly strength)   19 *for* on account of; *aspect* appearance   20 *proportion* size   21 *seely* frail   22 *writhled* shriveled   30 *Marry* (a mild interjection – originally an oath on the name of the Virgin Mary); *for that* because   31 *certify* inform   34 *trained* lured   35 *shadow* image, portrait; *thrall* slave

But now the substance shall endure the like,
And I will chain these legs and arms of thine
That hast by tyranny these many years   39
Wasted our country, slain our citizens,   40
And sent our sons and husbands captive –   41

TALBOT
Ha, ha, ha!

COUNTESS
Laughest thou, wretch? Thy mirth shall turn to moan.   43

TALBOT
I laugh to see your ladyship so fond   44
To think that you have aught but Talbot's shadow
Whereon to practice your severity.

COUNTESS
Why? Art not thou the man?

TALBOT
I am indeed.

COUNTESS
Then have I substance too.

TALBOT
No, no, I am but shadow of myself.   50
You are deceived; my substance is not here.
For what you see is but the smallest part   52
And least proportion of humanity.
I tell you, madam, were the whole frame here,   54
It is of such a spacious lofty pitch   55
Your roof were not sufficient to contain't.

COUNTESS
This is a riddling merchant for the nonce.   57
He will be here, and yet he is not here.
How can these contrarieties agree?

---

39 *tyranny* cruelty **41** *captive* made prisoner **43** *moan* lamentation **44** *fond* foolish **52–53** *what . . . humanity* (1) the body is the least significant part of the whole of man, (2) I am a mere fraction of my army **54** *frame* (1) structure of man, (2) engine (i.e., his army) **55** *pitch* height **57** *riddling merchant* riddlemonger; *nonce* occasion

TALBOT

60   That will I show you presently.

> *He winds his horn. Within, drums strike up; a peal of*
> *ordnance.*
> *Enter English Soldiers.*

How say you, madam? Are you now persuaded
That Talbot is but shadow of himself?
These are his substance, sinews, arms, and strength,
With which he yoketh your rebellious necks,

65   Razeth your cities and subverts your towns,
And in a moment makes them desolate.

COUNTESS

67   Victorious Talbot, pardon my abuse.

68   I find thou art no less than fame hath bruited,
And more than may be gathered by thy shape.

70   Let my presumption not provoke thy wrath,
For I am sorry that with reverence

72   I did not entertain thee as thou art.

TALBOT

73   Be not dismayed, fair lady, nor misconster
The mind of Talbot, as you did mistake
The outward composition of his body.
What you have done hath not offended me;
Nor other satisfaction do I crave

78   But only, with your patience, that we may

79   Taste of your wine and see what cates you have:

80   For soldiers' stomachs always serve them well.

COUNTESS

With all my heart; and think me honorèd
To feast so great a warrior in my house.   *Exeunt.*

*

---

60 *presently* immediately; **s.d.** *winds* blows; *peal of ordnance* salute of artillery
65 *subverts* overthrows   67 *abuse* (1) deceiving you, (2) self-delusion   68
fame report; *bruited* announced   72 *entertain* receive   73 *misconster* mis-
construe   78 *patience* permission   79 *cates* delicacies   80 *stomachs* (1) ap-
petites, (2) courage

∾ **II.4** *A rose brier. Enter Richard Plantagenet, the Earl of Warwick, the Duke of Somerset, William de la Pole (the Earl of Suffolk), Vernon, and a Lawyer.*

RICHARD PLANTAGENET
Great lords and gentlemen, what means this silence?
Dare no man answer in a case of truth?

SUFFOLK
Within the Temple hall we were too loud.   3
The garden here is more convenient.   4

RICHARD PLANTAGENET
Then say at once if I maintained the truth;   5
Or else was wrangling Somerset in th' error?

SUFFOLK
Faith, I have been a truant in the law,   7
And never yet could frame my will to it,   8
And therefore frame the law unto my will.

SOMERSET
Judge you, my Lord of Warwick, then between us.   10

WARWICK
Between two hawks, which flies the higher pitch, 11
Between two dogs, which hath the deeper mouth,   12
Between two blades, which bears the better temper,
Between two horses, which doth bear him best,   14
Between two girls, which hath the merriest eye,
I have perhaps some shallow spirit of judgment;
But in these nice sharp quillets of the law,   17
Good faith, I am no wiser than a daw.   18

II.4 The Temple garden, near the Middle and Inner Temples, London   **3, 4**
Temple hall, garden (the Wars of the Roses are imagined as beginning in a quarrel among young aristocrats studying law at the Inns of Court)   **3** *were* would have been   **5–6** *Then . . . error* i.e., heads I win, tails you lose   **7** *a truant* neglectful of study   **8** *frame* adapt   **11** *pitch* elevation   **12** *mouth* bark   **14** *bear him* carry himself   **17** *nice sharp quillets* fine subtle distinctions   **18** *daw* jackdaw (proverbially a stupid bird)

RICHARD PLANTAGENET
Tut, tut, here is a mannerly forbearance.
20 The truth appears so naked on my side
21 That any purblind eye may find it out.

SOMERSET
And on my side it is so well appareled,
So clear, so shining, and so evident,
That it will glimmer through a blind man's eye.

RICHARD PLANTAGENET
Since you are tongue-tied and so loath to speak,
26 In dumb significants proclaim your thoughts.
Let him that is a true-born gentleman
28 And stands upon the honor of his birth,
29 If he suppose that I have pleaded truth,
30 From off this brier pluck a white rose with me.
He plucks a white rose.

SOMERSET
Let him that is no coward nor no flatterer,
32 But dare maintain the party of the truth,
Pluck a red rose from off this thorn with me.
He plucks a red rose.

WARWICK
34 I love no colors, and without all color
Of base insinuating flattery
I pluck this white rose with Plantagenet.

SUFFOLK
I pluck this red rose with young Somerset,
38 And say withal I think he held the right.

VERNON
Stay, lords and gentlemen, and pluck no more
40 Till you conclude that he upon whose side
The fewest roses from the tree are cropped

---

21 *purblind* partially blind   26 *dumb significants* silent symbols   28 *stands
upon* insists on   29 *pleaded* argued (one of many legal terms in this scene)
32 *party* side in a legal case   34 *color* semblance   38 *withal* besides

Shall yield the other in the right opinion.   42
SOMERSET
    Good Master Vernon, it is well objected.   43
    If I have fewest, I subscribe in silence.   44
RICHARD PLANTAGENET
    And I.
VERNON
    Then for the truth and plainness of the case
    I pluck this pale and maiden blossom here,
    Giving my verdict on the white rose' side.
SOMERSET
    Prick not your finger as you pluck it off,
    Lest, bleeding, you do paint the white rose red,   50
    And fall on my side so against your will.
VERNON
    If I, my lord, for my opinion bleed,   52
    Opinion shall be surgeon to my hurt   53
    And keep me on the side where still I am.
SOMERSET
    Well, well, come on! Who else?
LAWYER
    Unless my study and my books be false,
    The argument you held was wrong in law;
    In sign whereof I pluck a white rose too.
RICHARD PLANTAGENET
    Now Somerset, where is your argument?
SOMERSET
    Here in my scabbard, meditating that   60
    Shall dye your white rose in a bloody red.
RICHARD PLANTAGENET
    Meantime your cheeks do counterfeit our roses,   62
    For pale they look with fear, as witnessing

---

42 *yield* concede (at law) 43 *objected* urged, brought forward (at law) 44
subscribe concur (literally, sign at the bottom of a document) 52 *opinion*
conviction 53 *Opinion* reputation 60 *meditating that* thinking of what
62 *counterfeit* imitate

The truth on our side.

SOMERSET   No, Plantagenet,
'Tis not for fear, but anger, that thy cheeks
Blush for pure shame to counterfeit our roses,
And yet thy tongue will not confess thy error.

RICHARD PLANTAGENET
68   Hath not thy rose a canker, Somerset?

SOMERSET
Hath not thy rose a thorn, Plantagenet?

RICHARD PLANTAGENET
70   Ay, sharp and piercing, to maintain his truth,
Whiles thy consuming canker eats his falsehood.

SOMERSET
Well, I'll find friends to wear my bleeding roses,
That shall maintain what I have said is true,
Where false Plantagenet dare not be seen.

RICHARD PLANTAGENET
Now, by this maiden blossom in my hand,
76   I scorn thee and thy fashion, peevish boy.

SUFFOLK
Turn not thy scorns this way, Plantagenet.

RICHARD PLANTAGENET
78   Proud Pole, I will, and scorn both him and thee.

SUFFOLK
I'll turn my part thereof into thy throat.

SOMERSET
80   Away, away, good William de la Pole.
81   We grace the yeoman by conversing with him.

WARWICK
Now, by God's will, thou wrong'st him, Somerset.
83   His grandfather was Lionel Duke of Clarence,
Third son to the third Edward, King of England.

---

68 *canker* cankerworm (a caterpillar that feeds on buds and leaves)   70 *his* its   76 *fashion* i.e., of wearing red roses   78 *Pole* (Suffolk's family name, as in l. 80)   81 *grace* honor; *yeoman* freeholder below rank of gentleman (Plantagenet lost his lands and titles when his father was executed for treason by Henry V)   83 *grandfather* (actually, great-great-grandfather)

Spring crestless yeomen from so deep a root?   85

RICHARD PLANTAGENET

He bears him on the place's privilege,   86
Or durst not for his craven heart say thus.   87

SOMERSET

By him that made me, I'll maintain my words
On any plot of ground in Christendom.
Was not thy father, Richard Earl of Cambridge,   90
For treason executed in our late king's days?
And by his treason stand'st not thou attainted,   92
Corrupted, and exempt from ancient gentry?   93
His trespass yet lives guilty in thy blood,
And till thou be restored thou art a yeoman.   95

RICHARD PLANTAGENET

My father was attachèd, not attainted;   96
Condemned to die for treason, but no traitor –
And that I'll prove on better men than Somerset,
Were growing time once ripened to my will.
For your partaker Pole, and you yourself,   100
I'll note you in my book of memory,
To scourge you for this apprehension.   102
Look to it well, and say you are well warned.

SOMERSET

Ah, thou shalt find us ready for thee still,
And know us by these colors for thy foes,
For these my friends, in spite of thee, shall wear.

RICHARD PLANTAGENET

And, by my soul, this pale and angry rose,

---

85 *crestless* (1) lacking heraldic crest, (2) cowardly   **86** *bears . . . privilege* i.e., presumes upon the legal asylum of the Inns of Court (granted them as ancient religious houses and as courts of law)   **87** *craven* cowardly   **92–93** *attainted, / Corrupted* (the legal effects of a bill of attainder were to deprive the culprit's descendants of title)   **93** *exempt* excluded; *gentry* rank of gentlemen   **95** *restored* given back lands and titles   **96** *attachèd, not attainted* (as Plantagenet insists, his father was actually arrested and executed summarily for treason by order of Henry V, and not by a full bill of attainder in Parliament; he implies that perfect justice was not done)   **100** *partaker* part taker, ally   **102** *apprehension* opinion

108 As cognizance of my blood-drinking hate,
    Will I for ever, and my faction, wear
110 Until it wither with me to my grave,
111 Or flourish to the height of my degree.

SUFFOLK
    Go forward, and be choked with thy ambition.
    And so farewell until I meet thee next.   *Exit.*

SOMERSET
114 Have with thee, Pole. – Farewell, ambitious Richard.
                                                           Exit.

RICHARD PLANTAGENET
115 How I am braved, and must perforce endure it!

WARWICK
116 This blot that they object against your house
    Shall be wiped out in the next parliament,
    Called for the truce of Winchester and Gloucester.
119 An if thou be not then created York,
120 I will not live to be accounted Warwick.
121 Meantime, in signal of my love to thee,
    Against proud Somerset and William Pole,
    Will I upon thy party wear this rose.
    And here I prophesy: this brawl today,
125 Grown to this faction in the Temple garden,
    Shall send, between the red rose and the white,
    A thousand souls to death and deadly night.

RICHARD PLANTAGENET
    Good Master Vernon, I am bound to you,
    That you on my behalf would pluck a flower.

VERNON
130 In your behalf still will I wear the same.

LAWYER
    And so will I.

---

108 *cognizance* badge   111 *degree* noble rank   114 *Have with thee* let us go
115 *braved* insulted   116 *object* allege   119 *An if* if   121 *signal* token   125
faction conflict

RICHARD PLANTAGENET
　Thanks, gentles.
　Come, let us four to dinner. I dare say
　This quarrel will drink blood another day.
　　　　　　　　　Exeunt. The rose brier is removed.

　　　　　　　*

❧ **II.5** *Enter Edmund Mortimer, brought in a chair by
　his Keepers.*

MORTIMER
　Kind keepers of my weak decaying age,
　Let dying Mortimer here rest himself.
　Even like a man new-halèd from the rack,   3
　So fare my limbs with long imprisonment;
　And these gray locks, the pursuivants of death,   5
　Argue the end of Edmund Mortimer,   6
　Nestor-like agèd in an age of care.   7
　These eyes, like lamps whose wasting oil is spent,
　Wax dim, as drawing to their exigent;   9
　Weak shoulders, overborne with burdening grief,   10
　And pithless arms, like to a withered vine   11
　That droops his sapless branches to the ground.   12
　Yet are these feet – whose strengthless stay is numb,   13
　Unable to support this lump of clay –
　Swift-wingèd with desire to get a grave,
　As witting I no other comfort have.   16
　But tell me, keeper, will my nephew come?
KEEPER
　Richard Plantagenet, my lord, will come.
　We sent unto the Temple, unto his chamber,
　And answer was returned that he will come.   20

————
II.5 A cell within the Tower of London **3** *new-halèd* recently dragged **5** *pursuivants* heralds **6** *Argue* portend **7** *Nestor* aged Greek leader in the Trojan War **9** *exigent* end **11** *pithless* strengthless **12** *his* its **13** *stay is numb* support is powerless **16** *As witting* as if they knew

MORTIMER
    Enough. My soul shall then be satisfied.
22   Poor gentleman, his wrong doth equal mine.
23   Since Henry Monmouth first began to reign –
    Before whose glory I was great in arms –
25   This loathsome sequestration have I had;
    And even since then hath Richard been obscured,
    Deprived of honor and inheritance.
    But now the arbitrator of despairs,
    Just Death, kind umpire of men's miseries,
30   With sweet enlargement doth dismiss me hence.
31   I would his troubles likewise were expired,
    That so he might recover what was lost.
       Enter Richard Plantagenet.

KEEPER
    My lord, your loving nephew now is come.

MORTIMER
    Richard Plantagenet, my friend, is he come?

RICHARD PLANTAGENET
    Ay, noble uncle, thus ignobly used:
36   Your nephew, late despisèd Richard, comes.

MORTIMER   *To Keepers*
    Direct mine arms I may embrace his neck
38   And in his bosom spend my latter gasp.
    O tell me when my lips do touch his cheeks,
40   That I may kindly give one fainting kiss.
       He embraces Richard.
41   And now declare, sweet stem from York's great stock,
    Why didst thou say of late thou wert despised?

RICHARD PLANTAGENET
    First lean thine agèd back against mine arm,
44   And in that ease I'll tell thee my dis-ease.

---

22 *his wrong* i.e., the wrong done him   23 *Henry Monmouth* Henry V   25 *sequestration* isolation, loss of property and freedom   30 *enlargement* freedom   31 *his* i.e., Richard's; *expired* ended   36 *late* recently   38 *latter* final   40 *kindly* (1) affectionately, (2) to a kinsman   41 *stem, stock* (from the metaphor of the genealogical tree)   44 *dis-ease* grievance

This day in argument upon a case   45
Some words there grew 'twixt Somerset and me;
Among which terms he used his lavish tongue
And did upbraid me with my father's death;
Which obloquy set bars before my tongue,   49
Else with the like I had requited him.   50
Therefore, good uncle, for my father's sake,
In honor of a true Plantagenet,
And for alliance' sake, declare the cause   53
My father, Earl of Cambridge, lost his head.

MORTIMER
That cause, fair nephew, that imprisoned me,
And hath detained me all my flow'ring youth
Within a loathsome dungeon, there to pine,
Was cursèd instrument of his decease.

RICHARD PLANTAGENET
Discover more at large what cause that was,   59
For I am ignorant and cannot guess.   60

MORTIMER
I will, if that my fading breath permit
And death approach not ere my tale be done.
Henry the Fourth, grandfather to this king,
Deposed his nephew Richard, Edward's son,   64
The first-begotten and the lawful heir
Of Edward king, the third of that descent;
During whose reign the Percies of the north,   67
Finding his usurpation most unjust,
Endeavored my advancement to the throne.
The reason moved these warlike lords to this   70
Was for that – young King Richard thus removed,   71
Leaving no heir begotten of his body –

---

45 *This day* (Plantagenet has come to the Tower prison directly after his argument in the Temple garden, to find out more about his father's disgrace) **49** *obloquy* disgrace   **53** *alliance'* kinship's   **59** *Discover* expound; *at large* fully   **64** *nephew* blood relative (here, first cousin)   **67** *whose* i.e., Henry IV's   **70** *moved* that moved   **71** *for that* because

73   I was the next by birth and parentage,
74   For by my mother I derivèd am
       From Lionel Duke of Clarence, the third son
       To King Edward the Third – whereas the king
       From John of Gaunt doth bring his pedigree,
       Being but fourth of that heroic line.
79   But mark: as in this haughty great attempt
80   They laborèd to plant the rightful heir,
       I lost my liberty, and they their lives.
       Long after this, when Henry the Fifth,
       Succeeding his father Bolingbroke, did reign,
       Thy father, Earl of Cambridge then, derived
       From famous Edmund Langley, Duke of York,
       Marrying my sister that thy mother was,
       Again, in pity of my hard distress,
88   Levied an army, weening to redeem
       And have installed me in the diadem;
90   But, as the rest, so fell that noble earl,
       And was beheaded. Thus the Mortimers,
       In whom the title rested, were suppressed.

RICHARD PLANTAGENET
       Of which, my lord, your honor is the last.

MORTIMER
       True, and thou seest that I no issue have,
95   And that my fainting words do warrant death.
96   Thou art my heir. The rest I wish thee gather –
       But yet be wary in thy studious care.

RICHARD PLANTAGENET
       Thy grave admonishments prevail with me.
       But yet methinks my father's execution
100   Was nothing less than bloody tyranny.

MORTIMER
101   With silence, nephew, be thou politic.

---

73 *next* i.e., in line for the throne   74 *derivèd* descended   79 *haughty* lofty
88 *weening* intending   95 *warrant* assure   96 *gather* (1) infer, (2) collect
101 *politic* prudent

Strong-fixèd is the house of Lancaster,
And like a mountain, not to be removed.
But now thy uncle is removing hence,   104
As princes do their courts, when they are cloyed   105
With long continuance in a settled place.

RICHARD PLANTAGENET
O uncle, would some part of my young years
Might but redeem the passage of your age.   108

MORTIMER
Thou dost then wrong me, as that slaughterer doth
Which giveth many wounds when one will kill.   *110*
Mourn not, except thou sorrow for my good.   111
Only give order for my funeral.   112
And so farewell, and fair be all thy hopes,
And prosperous be thy life in peace and war.
    Dies.

RICHARD PLANTAGENET
And peace, no war, befall thy parting soul.
In prison hast thou spent a pilgrimage,
And like a hermit overpassed thy days.   117
Well, I will lock his counsel in my breast,
And what I do imagine, let that rest.   119
Keepers, convey him hence, and I myself   *120*
Will see his burial better than his life.
                    Exeunt Keepers with Mortimer's body.
Here dies the dusky torch of Mortimer,
Choked with ambition of the meaner sort.   123
And for those wrongs, those bitter injuries,   124
Which Somerset hath offered to my house,
I doubt not but with honor to redress.
And therefore haste I to the parliament,

---

104 *removing* departing   105 *cloyed* sickened   108 *redeem* buy back   **111**
except unless   112 *give order* make arrangements   117 *overpassed* spent
119 *let that rest* leave that alone   123 *the meaner sort* people of inferior rank
(i.e., Bolingbroke and his family)   124 *And for* and as for

128   Either to be restorèd to my blood,
129   Or make mine ill th' advantage of my good.   *Exit.*

*

❧ **III.1** *Flourish. Enter young King Henry, the Dukes of Exeter and Gloucester, the Bishop of Winchester; the Duke of Somerset and the Earl of Suffolk with red roses; the Earl of Warwick and Richard Plantagenet with white roses. Gloucester offers to put up a bill; Winchester snatches it, tears it.*

BISHOP OF WINCHESTER
      Com'st thou with deep premeditated lines?
      With written pamphlets studiously devised?
      Humphrey of Gloucester, if thou canst accuse,
      Or aught intend'st to lay unto my charge,
5   Do it without invention, suddenly,
      As I with sudden and extemporal speech
7   Purpose to answer what thou canst object.
GLOUCESTER
8   Presumptuous priest, this place commands my pa-
         tience,
      Or thou shouldst find thou hast dishonored me.
10   Think not, although in writing I preferred
      The manner of thy vile outrageous crimes,
      That therefore I have forged, or am not able
13   Verbatim to rehearse the method of my pen.
      No, prelate, such is thy audacious wickedness,
15   Thy lewd, pestiferous, and dissentious pranks,
16   As very infants prattle of thy pride.

---

128 *blood* hereditary rights   **129** *make . . . good* make some opportunity for advancement out of my sheer determination
      III.1 The Parliament House, London **s.d.** *put up a bill* present an indictment   **5** *invention* premeditation; *suddenly* extempore   **7** *object* urge, argue   **8** *this place* i.e., Parliament   **10** *preferred* set out   **13** *Verbatim* orally; *rehearse . . . pen* recount the sum of what I have written   **15** *lewd* wicked   **16** *As very* that even

Thou art a most pernicious usurer,
Froward by nature, enemy to peace,   18
Lascivious, wanton, more than well beseems
A man of thy profession and degree.   20
And for thy treachery, what's more manifest? –   21
In that thou laid'st a trap to take my life,
As well at London Bridge as at the Tower.
Beside, I fear me, if thy thoughts were sifted,   24
The king thy sovereign is not quite exempt
From envious malice of thy swelling heart.

BISHOP OF WINCHESTER
Gloucester, I do defy thee. – Lords, vouchsafe
To give me hearing what I shall reply.
If I were covetous, ambitious, or perverse,
As he will have me, how am I so poor?   30
Or how haps it I seek not to advance
Or raise myself, but keep my wonted calling?   32
And for dissension, who preferreth peace
More than I do? – except I be provoked.   34
No, my good lords, it is not that offends;   35
It is not that that hath incensed the duke.
It is because no one should sway but he,   37
No one but he should be about the king –
And that engenders thunder in his breast
And makes him roar these accusations forth.   40
But he shall know I am as good –

GLOUCESTER
As good? –
Thou bastard of my grandfather.   43

BISHOP OF WINCHESTER
Ay, lordly sir; for what are you, I pray,
But one imperious in another's throne?   45

---

18 *Froward* perverse   20 *degree* rank   21 *And for* and as for   24 *sifted*
closely examined   32 *wonted* customary   34 *except* unless   35 *that* that
which   37 *sway* rule   43 *my grandfather* John of Ghent (pronounced
"Gaunt"), who fathered the illegitimate Beauforts by his mistress, Catherine
Swynford   45 *imperious* ruling

GLOUCESTER
Am I not Protector, saucy priest?

BISHOP OF WINCHESTER
And am not I a prelate of the church?

GLOUCESTER
48 Yes — as an outlaw in a castle keeps
49 And useth it to patronage his theft.

BISHOP OF WINCHESTER
50 Unreverent Gloucester.

GLOUCESTER   Thou art reverend
51 Touching thy spiritual function, not thy life.

BISHOP OF WINCHESTER
Rome shall remedy this.

GLOUCESTER   Roam thither then.

WARWICK   *To Winchester*
My lord, it were your duty to forbear.

SOMERSET
54 Ay, so the bishop be not overborne:
55 Methinks my lord should be religious,
56 And know the office that belongs to such.

WARWICK
57 Methinks his lordship should be humbler.
58 It fitteth not a prelate so to plead.

SOMERSET
59 Yes, when his holy state is touched so near.

WARWICK
60 State holy or unhallowed, what of that?
Is not his grace Protector to the king?

RICHARD PLANTAGENET   *Aside*
Plantagenet, I see, must hold his tongue,
Lest it be said, "Speak, sirrah, when you should;
64 Must your bold verdict intertalk with lords?"

---

48 *keeps* dwells   49 *patronage* maintain   51 *Touching . . . function* i.e., in
title only   54 *so* as long as; *overborne* overruled   55 *my lord* i.e., Gloucester;
religious pious   56 *office* duty; *such* i.e., prelates   57 *his lordship* i.e., Winchester   58 *plead* wrangle   59 *holy . . . near* high ecclesiastical status is af-
fected so directly   64 *verdict* opinion; *intertalk* converse

Else would I have a fling at Winchester.

KING HENRY
  Uncles of Gloucester and of Winchester,
  The special watchmen of our English weal,   67
  I would prevail, if prayers might prevail,
  To join your hearts in love and amity.
  O what a scandal is it to our crown   70
  That two such noble peers as ye should jar!   71
  Believe me, lords, my tender years can tell
  Civil dissension is a viperous worm
  That gnaws the bowels of the commonwealth.
    A noise within.

SERVINGMEN   *Within*
  Down with the tawny coats!

KING HENRY
  What tumult's this?

WARWICK   An uproar, I dare warrant,
  Begun through malice of the bishop's men.
    A noise again.

SERVINGMEN   *Within*
  Stones, stones!
    Enter the Mayor of London.

MAYOR
  O my good lords, and virtuous Henry,
  Pity the city of London, pity us!   80
  The bishop and the Duke of Gloucester's men,   81
  Forbidden late to carry any weapon,   82
  Have filled their pockets full of pebble stones
  And, banding themselves in contrary parts,   84
  Do pelt so fast at one another's pate
  That many have their giddy brains knocked out.
  Our windows are broke down in every street,
  And we for fear compelled to shut our shops.

---

67 *weal* (1) well-being, (2) state **71** *jar* quarrel **81** *bishop* i.e., bishop's **82**
late lately **84** *contrary parts* opposing factions

Enter in skirmish, with bloody pates, Bishop Beaufort's
Servingmen in tawny coats and Gloucester's in blue
coats.

KING HENRY
 We charge you, on allegiance to ourself,
90 To hold your slaught'ring hands and keep the peace.
  The skirmish ceases.
 Pray, uncle Gloucester, mitigate this strife.

FIRST SERVINGMAN Nay, if we be forbidden stones, we'll
 fall to it with our teeth.

SECOND SERVINGMAN
 Do what ye dare, we are as resolute.
  Skirmish again.

GLOUCESTER
95 You of my household, leave this peevish broil,
96 And set this unaccustomed fight aside.

THIRD SERVINGMAN
 My lord, we know your grace to be a man
 Just and upright and, for your royal birth,
 Inferior to none but to his majesty;
100 And ere that we will suffer such a prince,
 So kind a father of the commonweal,
102 To be disgracèd by an inkhorn mate,
 We and our wives and children all will fight
 And have our bodies slaughtered by thy foes.

FIRST SERVINGMAN
 Ay, and the very parings of our nails
106 Shall pitch a field when we are dead.
  They begin to skirmish again.

GLOUCESTER   Stay, stay, I say!
 An if you love me as you say you do,

---

95 *peevish* senseless 96 *unaccustomed* (1) unusual, (2) contrary to good cus-
tom 100 *ere that* before 102 *disgracèd* insulted; *inkhorn mate* scribbler,
low pedant 106 *pitch a field* drive in sharp stakes to protect against cavalry

Let me persuade you to forbear a while.
KING HENRY
  O how this discord doth afflict my soul!
  Can you, my Lord of Winchester, behold   110
  My sighs and tears, and will not once relent?
  Who should be pitiful if you be not?   112
  Or who should study to prefer a peace,   113
  If holy churchmen take delight in broils?
WARWICK
  Yield, my Lord Protector; yield, Winchester –
  Except you mean with obstinate repulse   116
  To slay your sovereign and destroy the realm.
  You see what mischief – and what murder, too –
  Hath been enacted through your enmity.
  Then be at peace, except ye thirst for blood.   120
BISHOP OF WINCHESTER
  He shall submit, or I will never yield.
GLOUCESTER
  Compassion on the king commands me stoop,
  Or I would see his heart out ere the priest
  Should ever get that privilege of me.   124
WARWICK
  Behold, my Lord of Winchester, the duke
  Hath banished moody discontented fury,   126
  As by his smoothèd brows it doth appear.
  Why look you still so stern and tragical?
GLOUCESTER
  Here, Winchester, I offer thee my hand.
KING HENRY   *To Winchester*
  Fie, uncle Beaufort! I have heard you preach   130
  That malice was a great and grievous sin;
  And will not you maintain the thing you teach,
  But prove a chief offender in the same?

---

112 *pitiful* merciful   113 *prefer* assist in bringing about   116 *Except* unless;
repulse refusal   124 *privilege of* advantage yielded by   126 *moody* haughty

WARWICK
134   Sweet king! The bishop hath a kindly gird.
     For shame, my Lord of Winchester, relent.
     What, shall a child instruct you what to do?

BISHOP OF WINCHESTER
     Well, Duke of Gloucester, I will yield to thee
     Love for thy love, and hand for hand I give.

GLOUCESTER   *Aside*
139   Ay, but I fear me with a hollow heart.
       To the others
140   See here, my friends and loving countrymen,
     This token serveth for a flag of truce
     Betwixt ourselves and all our followers.
     So help me God, as I dissemble not.

BISHOP OF WINCHESTER
     So help me God – *(Aside)* as I intend it not.

KING HENRY
     O loving uncle, kind Duke of Gloucester,
     How joyful am I made by this contract!
       To Servingmen
147   Away, my masters, trouble us no more,
     But join in friendship as your lords have done.

FIRST SERVINGMAN
     Content. I'll to the surgeon's.

SECOND SERVINGMAN
150   And so will I.

151 THIRD SERVINGMAN   And I will see what physic the tav-
     ern affords.   *Exeunt the Mayor and Servingmen.*

WARWICK
     Accept this scroll, most gracious sovereign,
     Which in the right of Richard Plantagenet
     We do exhibit to your majesty.

GLOUCESTER
     Well urged, my Lord of Warwick – for, sweet prince,

---

134 *kindly gird* proper rebuke   **139** *hollow* insincere   **147** *masters* (condescending term for servants)   **151** *physic* remedy

An if your grace mark every circumstance,   157
You have great reason to do Richard right,
Especially for those occasions   159
At Eltham Place I told your majesty.   160

KING HENRY
And those occasions, uncle, were of force. –
Therefore, my loving lords, our pleasure is
That Richard be restorèd to his blood.   163

WARWICK
Let Richard be restorèd to his blood.
So shall his father's wrongs be recompensed.   165

BISHOP OF WINCHESTER
As will the rest, so willeth Winchester.

KING HENRY
If Richard will be true, not that alone   167
But all the whole inheritance I give
That doth belong unto the house of York,
From whence you spring by lineal descent.   170

RICHARD PLANTAGENET
Thy humble servant vows obedience
And humble service till the point of death.

KING HENRY
Stoop then, and set your knee against my foot.
    Richard kneels.
And in reguerdon of that duty done,   174
I gird thee with the valiant sword of York.
Rise, Richard, like a true Plantagenet,
And rise created princely Duke of York.

RICHARD DUKE OF YORK   *Rising*
And so thrive Richard, as thy foes may fall;
And as my duty springs, so perish they
That grudge one thought against your majesty.   180

---

157 *An if* if   159 *occasions* circumstances   163 *restorèd . . . blood* i.e., rein-
stated in the inherited titles forfeited by his father   165 *recompensed* com-
pensated   167 *true* loyal   174 *reguerdon* reward

ALL BUT RICHARD AND SOMERSET
    Welcome, high prince, the mighty Duke of York!
SOMERSET *Aside*
    Perish, base prince, ignoble Duke of York!
GLOUCESTER
    Now will it best avail your majesty
    To cross the seas and to be crowned in France.
    The presence of a king engenders love
    Amongst his subjects and his loyal friends,
187   As it disanimates his enemies.
KING HENRY
    When Gloucester says the word, King Henry goes,
    For friendly counsel cuts off many foes.
GLOUCESTER
190   Your ships already are in readiness.
                            Sennet. Exeunt all but Exeter.

EXETER
    Ay, we may march in England or in France,
    Not seeing what is likely to ensue.
193   This late dissension grown betwixt the peers
    Burns under feignèd ashes of forged love,
    And will at last break out into a flame.
196   As festered members rot but by degree
    Till bones and flesh and sinews fall away,
    So will this base and envious discord breed.
    And now I fear that fatal prophecy
200   Which, in the time of Henry named the Fifth,
    Was in the mouth of every sucking babe:
202   That "Henry born at Monmouth should win all,
203   And Henry born at Windsor should lose all" –
    Which is so plain that Exeter doth wish
    His days may finish, ere that hapless time.   *Exit.*
                            *

---

187 *disanimates* discourages 190 s.d. *Sennet* trumpet notes that accompany
a procession 193 *late* recent 196 *members* parts of the body 202
Henry . . . Monmouth Henry V 203 *Henry . . . Windsor* Henry VI

ᴼᴼ **III.2** *Enter Joan la Pucelle, disguised, with four*
  French Soldiers with sacks upon their backs.

JOAN
  These are the city gates, the gates of Rouen,   1
  Through which our policy must make a breach.   2
  Take heed. Be wary how you place your words.   3
  Talk like the vulgar sort of marketmen   4
  That come to gather money for their corn.   5
  If we have entrance, as I hope we shall,
  And that we find the slothful watch but weak,   7
  I'll by a sign give notice to our friends,
  That Charles the Dauphin may encounter them.
SOLDIER
  Our sacks shall be a mean to sack the city,   10
  And we be lords and rulers over Rouen.
  Therefore we'll knock.
      They knock.
WATCH   *Within*
    Qui là?   13
JOAN   *Paysans, la pauvre gens de France:*
  Poor market folks that come to sell their corn.
WATCH   *Opening the gates*
  Enter, go in. The market bell is rung.
JOAN   *Aside*
  Now, Rouen, I'll shake thy bulwarks to the ground.
                                                Exeunt.

                            *

III.2 In and around Rouen, France **1** *Rouen* (spelled and pronounced in
Elizabethan times "Roan," a monosyllable) **2** *policy* stratagem **3** *place*
arrange **4** *vulgar* common (not disparaging) **5** *corn* wheat **7** *that* if **10**
mean means **13** *Qui là?* who's there; *Paysans . . . France* peasants, the poor
folk of France

ᔕ **III.3** *Enter Charles the Dauphin, the Bastard of*
Orléans, the Duke of Alençon, René Duke of Anjou,
and French Soldiers.

CHARLES
    Saint Denis bless this happy stratagem,
    And once again we'll sleep secure in Rouen.
BASTARD
3   Here entered Pucelle and her practisants.
    Now she is there, how will she specify
    "Here is the best and safest passage in"?
RENÉ
    By thrusting out a torch from yonder tower –
    Which, once discerned, shows that her meaning is:
8   No way to that, for weakness, which she entered.
      Enter Joan la Pucelle on the top, thrusting out a torch
      burning.
JOAN
    Behold, this is the happy wedding torch
10   That joineth Rouen unto her countrymen,
11   But burning fatal to the Talbonites.
BASTARD
    See, noble Charles, the beacon of our friend.
    The burning torch in yonder turret stands.
CHARLES
14   Now shine it like a comet of revenge,
15   A prophet to the fall of all our foes!
RENÉ
    Defer no time; delays have dangerous ends.
17   Enter and cry "The dauphin!" presently,
    And then do execution on the watch.
                            Alarum. Exeunt.

III.3 In and around Rouen **3** *practisants* conspirators **8** *No . . . weakness*
i.e., no way compares in weakness with that **11** *Talbonites* followers of
Talbot **14** *shine it* may it shine **15** *A prophet* an omen **17** *presently* immediately

*

∾ **III.4** *An alarum. Enter Lord Talbot in an excursion.*

TALBOT
  France, thou shalt rue this treason with thy tears,
  If Talbot but survive thy treachery.
  Pucelle, that witch, that damnèd sorceress,
  Hath wrought this hellish mischief unawares,   4
  That hardly we escaped the pride of France.   *Exit.* 5

*

∾ **III.5** *An alarum. Excursions.*
  The Duke of Bedford brought in, sick, in a chair.
  Enter Lord Talbot and the Duke of Burgundy, with-
  out; within, Joan la Pucelle, Charles the Dauphin, the
  Bastard of Orléans, the Duke of Alençon, and René
  Duke of Anjou on the walls.

JOAN
  Good morrow gallants. Want ye corn for bread?
  I think the Duke of Burgundy will fast
  Before he'll buy again at such a rate.
  'Twas full of darnel. Do you like the taste?   4
BURGUNDY
  Scoff on, vile fiend and shameless courtesan.
  I trust ere long to choke thee with thine own,   6
  And make thee curse the harvest of that corn.
CHARLES
  Your grace may starve, perhaps, before that time.
BEDFORD
  O let no words, but deeds, revenge this treason.

III.4 In and around Rouen **s.d.** *an excursion* a skirmish **4** *mischief unawares*
harm unexpectedly **5** *hardly* with difficulty; *pride* power
  III.5 In and around Rouen **4** *darnel* weeds **6** *thine own* your own bread

JOAN

10   What will you do, good graybeard? Break a lance
11   And run atilt at death within a chair?

TALBOT

12   Foul fiend of France, and hag of all despite,
     Encompassed with thy lustful paramours,
     Becomes it thee to taunt his valiant age
     And twit with cowardice a man half dead?
16   Damsel, I'll have a bout with you again,
     Or else let Talbot perish with this shame.

JOAN

18   Are ye so hot, sir? – Yet, Pucelle, hold thy peace.
     If Talbot do but thunder, rain will follow.
     The English whisper together in counsel.
20   God speed the parliament; who shall be the speaker?

TALBOT

     Dare ye come forth and meet us in the field?

JOAN

     Belike your lordship takes us then for fools,
     To try if that our own be ours or no.

TALBOT

24   I speak not to that railing Hecate
     But unto thee, Alençon, and the rest.
     Will ye, like soldiers, come and fight it out?

ALENÇON

27   Seignieur, no.

TALBOT   Seignieur, hang! Base muleteers of France,
28   Like peasant footboys do they keep the walls
     And dare not take up arms like gentlemen.

JOAN

30   Away, captains, let's get us from the walls,
     For Talbot means no goodness by his looks.

---

11 *run atilt at* joust with   **12** *of all despite* most despicable   **16** *bout* (1) fight, (2) sexual tussle   **18** *hot* (1) angry, (2) lustful   **24** *Hecate* goddess identified with the moon and the underworld (and hence as the guardian of witches)   **27** *Base muleteers* mule drivers of low birth   **28** *keep* stay near

Good-bye, my lord. We came but to tell you
That we are here.   *Exeunt French from the walls.*

TALBOT

And there will we be, too, ere it be long,
Or else reproach be Talbot's greatest fame.
Vow, Burgundy, by honor of thy house,
Pricked on by public wrongs sustained in France,   37
Either to get the town again or die.
And I – as sure as English Henry lives,
And as his father here was conqueror;   40
As sure as in this late betrayèd town   41
Great Coeur de Lion's heart was buried –   42
So sure I swear to get the town or die.

BURGUNDY

My vows are equal partners with thy vows.

TALBOT

But ere we go, regard this dying prince,   45
The valiant Duke of Bedford. *(To Bedford)* Come, my lord,
We will bestow you in some better place,
Fitter for sickness and for crazy age.   48

BEDFORD

Lord Talbot, do not so dishonor me.
Here will I sit before the walls of Rouen,   50
And will be partner of your weal or woe.

BURGUNDY

Courageous Bedford, let us now persuade you.

BEDFORD

Not to be gone from hence; for once I read
That stout Pendragon, in his litter sick,   54
Came to the field and vanquishèd his foes.

---

37 *Pricked on* goaded   40 *father . . . conqueror* (Henry V captured Rouen in
1418)   41 *late* recently   42 *Great . . . buried* (Richard I willed his heart to
be buried in Rouen as an expression of esteem for that city)   45 *regard* attend to   48 *crazy* decrepit   54–55 *Pendragon . . . foes* (told of Uther Pendragon's brother in his victory against the Saxons)

56 Methinks I should revive the soldiers' hearts
   Because I ever found them as myself.

TALBOT
   Undaunted spirit in a dying breast!
   Then be it so; heavens keep old Bedford safe.
60 And now no more ado, brave Burgundy,
61 But gather we our forces out of hand,
   And set upon our boasting enemy.

Exit with Burgundy.

*An alarum. Excursions. Enter Sir John Fastolf and a
Captain.*

CAPTAIN
   Whither away, Sir John Fastolf, in such haste?

FASTOLF
   Whither away? To save myself by flight.
65 We are like to have the overthrow again.

CAPTAIN
   What, will you fly, and leave Lord Talbot?

FASTOLF
   Ay, all the Talbots in the world, to save my life.   *Exit.*

CAPTAIN
   Cowardly knight, ill fortune follow thee!   *Exit.*
   Retreat. Excursions. Joan, Alençon, and Charles fly.

BEDFORD
   Now, quiet soul, depart when heaven please,
70 For I have seen our enemies' overthrow.
   What is the trust or strength of foolish man?
   They that of late were daring with their scoffs
73 Are glad and fain by flight to save themselves.

*Bedford dies, and is carried in
by two in his chair.*

✳

---

56 *Methinks* it seems to me   61 *out of hand* at once   65 *have the overthrow*
be defeated   73 *fain* well pleased

∾ **III.6** *An alarum. Enter Lord Talbot, the Duke of*
Burgundy, and the rest of the English Soldiers.

TALBOT
  Lost and recovered in a day again!
  This is a double honor, Burgundy;
  Yet heavens have glory for this victory!
BURGUNDY
  Warlike and martial Talbot, Burgundy
  Enshrines thee in his heart, and there erects
  Thy noble deeds as valor's monuments.
TALBOT
  Thanks, gentle duke. But where is Pucelle now?   7
  I think her old familiar is asleep.   8
  Now where's the Bastard's braves, and Charles his   9
    gleeks?
  What, all amort? Rouen hangs her head for grief   10
  That such a valiant company are fled.
  Now will we take some order in the town,   12
  Placing therein some expert officers,
  And then depart to Paris, to the king,
  For there young Henry with his nobles lie.   15
BURGUNDY
  What wills Lord Talbot pleaseth Burgundy.
TALBOT
  But yet, before we go, let's not forget
  The noble Duke of Bedford late deceased,
  But see his exequies fulfilled in Rouen.   19
  A braver soldier never couchèd lance;   20
  A gentler heart did never sway in court.

III.6 In and around Rouen   7 *gentle* noble   8 *old familiar* customary attendant demon (i.e., the devil)   9 *braves* bravado; *Charles his gleeks* Charles's
scoffs   10 *amort* sick to death, dispirited   12 *take some order* make arrangements   15 *lie* lives   19 *exequies* funeral rites   20 *couchèd* leveled (for attack)

> But kings and mightiest potentates must die,
> For that's the end of human misery.   *Exeunt.*

*

∾ **III.7** *Enter Charles the Dauphin, the Bastard of Orléans, the Duke of Alençon, Joan la Pucelle, and French Soldiers.*

JOAN

1   Dismay not, princes, at this accident,
     Nor grieve that Rouen is so recoverèd.
3   Care is no cure, but rather corrosive,
     For things that are not to be remedied.
5   Let frantic Talbot triumph for a while,
     And like a peacock sweep along his tail;
7   We'll pull his plumes and take away his train,
8   If Dauphin and the rest will be but ruled.

CHARLES

     We have been guided by thee hitherto,
10   And of thy cunning had no diffidence.
11   One sudden foil shall never breed distrust.

BASTARD   *To Joan*

12   Search out thy wit for secret policies,
     And we will make thee famous through the world.

ALENÇON   *To Joan*

     We'll set thy statue in some holy place
     And have thee reverenced like a blessèd saint.
16   Employ thee then, sweet virgin, for our good.

JOAN

     Then thus it must be; this doth Joan devise:
     By fair persuasions mixed with sugared words
     We will entice the Duke of Burgundy

III.7 Plains near Rouen **1** *accident* unforeseen event **3** *Care* sorrow; *corrosive* aggravating **5** *frantic* mad **7** *train* (1) army, (2) peacock's tail **8** *be but ruled* follow instructions **10** *cunning* skill in magic; *diffidence* distrust **11** *foil* repulse **12** *policies* stratagems **16** *Employ thee* exert thyself

To leave the Talbot and to follow us.   20
CHARLES
Ay, marry, sweeting, if we could do that   21
France were no place for Henry's warriors,
Nor should that nation boast it so with us,
But be extirpèd from our provinces.   24
ALENÇON
For ever should they be expulsed from France   25
And not have title of an earldom here.
JOAN
Your honors shall perceive how I will work
To bring this matter to the wishèd end.
     Drum sounds afar off.
Hark, by the sound of drum you may perceive
Their powers are marching unto Paris-ward.   30
     Here sound an English march.
There goes the Talbot, with his colors spread,   31
And all the troops of English after him.
     Here sound a French march.
Now in the rearward comes the duke and his;
Fortune in favor makes him lag behind.   34
Summon a parley. We will talk with him.
     Trumpets sound a parley.
CHARLES   *Calling*
A parley with the Duke of Burgundy!
     Enter the Duke of Burgundy.
BURGUNDY
Who craves a parley with the Burgundy!
JOAN
The princely Charles of France, thy countryman.
BURGUNDY
What sayst thou, Charles? – for I am marching hence.

---

21 *sweeting* i.e., sweet one (a lover's nickname)   24 *extirpèd* rooted out   25 *expulsed* expelled   30 *Paris-ward* toward Paris   31 *colors spread* flags unfurled   34 *in favor* benevolently

CHARLES
40   Speak, Pucelle, and enchant him with thy words.

JOAN
41   Brave Burgundy, undoubted hope of France,
      Stay. Let thy humble handmaid speak to thee.

BURGUNDY
      Speak on, but be not overtedious.

JOAN
      Look on thy country, look on fertile France,
      And see the cities and the towns defaced
      By wasting ruin of the cruel foe.
      As looks the mother on her lowly babe
48   When death doth close his tender-dying eyes,
      See, see the pining malady of France;
50   Behold the wounds, the most unnatural wounds,
      Which thou thyself hast given her woeful breast.
      O turn thy edgèd sword another way,
      Strike those that hurt, and hurt not those that help.
      One drop of blood drawn from thy country's bosom
      Should grieve thee more than streams of foreign gore.
      Return thee, therefore, with a flood of tears,
      And wash away thy country's stainèd spots.

BURGUNDY   *Aside*
      Either she hath bewitched me with her words,
      Or nature makes me suddenly relent.

JOAN
60   Besides, all French and France exclaims on thee,
61   Doubting thy birth and lawful progeny.
      Who join'st thou with but with a lordly nation
      That will not trust thee but for profit's sake?
      When Talbot hath set footing once in France
      And fashioned thee that instrument of ill,
      Who then but English Henry will be lord,

---

41 *undoubted* certain   48 *tender-dying* dying at a tender age   50 *unnatural*
against the law of kinship   60 *exclaims on* denounces   61 *progeny* ancestry

And thou be thrust out like a fugitive?
Call we to mind, and mark but this for proof:
Was not the Duke of Orléans thy foe?
And was he not in England prisoner?   70
But when they heard he was thine enemy
They set him free, without his ransom paid,
In spite of Burgundy and all his friends.
See, then, thou fight'st against thy countrymen,
And join'st with them will be thy slaughtermen.
Come, come, return; return, thou wandering lord,   76
Charles and the rest will take thee in their arms.

BURGUNDY *Aside*
I am vanquishèd. These haughty words of hers   78
Have battered me like roaring cannon shot
And made me almost yield upon my knees.   80
    To the others
Forgive me, country, and sweet countrymen;
And lords, accept this hearty kind embrace.
My forces and my power of men are yours.
So farewell, Talbot. I'll no longer trust thee.

JOAN
Done like a Frenchman – *(Aside)* turn and turn again.

CHARLES
Welcome, brave duke. Thy friendship makes us fresh.

BASTARD
And doth beget new courage in our breasts.

ALENÇON
Pucelle hath bravely played her part in this,   88
And doth deserve a coronet of gold.

CHARLES
Now let us on, my lords, and join our powers,   90
And seek how we may prejudice the foe.   *Exeunt.*   91

                        ✳

---

76 *wandering* erring 78 *haughty* lofty 88 *bravely* (1) courageously, (2)
splendidly 91 *prejudice* harm

❧ **III.8**   *Flourish. Enter King Henry, Humphrey Duke*
of Gloucester, the Bishop of Winchester, the Duke of
Exeter; Richard Duke of York, the Earl of Warwick,
and Vernon with white roses; the Earl of Suffolk,
the Duke of Somerset, and Basset with red roses.
To them, with his Soldiers, enter Lord Talbot.

TALBOT
    My gracious prince and honorable peers,
    Hearing of your arrival in this realm
    I have a while given truce unto my wars
4   To do my duty to my sovereign;
    In sign whereof, this arm that hath reclaimed
    To your obedience fifty fortresses,
    Twelve cities, and seven wallèd towns of strength,
8   Beside five hundred prisoners of esteem,
    Lets fall his sword before your highness' feet,
10 And with submissive loyalty of heart
    Ascribes the glory of his conquest got
    First to my God, and next unto your grace.
        He kneels.
KING HENRY
    Is this the Lord Talbot, uncle Gloucester,
    That hath so long been resident in France?
GLOUCESTER
    Yes, if it please your majesty, my liege.
KING HENRY   *To Talbot*
    Welcome, brave captain and victorious lord.
    When I was young – as yet I am not old –
    I do remember how my father said
    A stouter champion never handled sword.
20 Long since we were resolvèd of your truth,
    Your faithful service and your toil in war,
    Yet never have you tasted our reward,

III.8 The palace, Paris   **4** *duty* feudal obeisance   **8** *esteem* noble rank   **20**
we (the royal plural); *resolvèd* convinced; *truth* loyalty

Or been reguerdoned with so much as thanks,   23
Because till now we never saw your face.
Therefore stand up,
  (Talbot rises.)   and for these good deserts
We here create you Earl of Shrewsbury;
And in our coronation take your place.
                    Sennet. Exeunt all but Vernon and Basset.

VERNON
Now sir, to you that were so hot at sea,   28
Disgracing of these colors that I wear   29
In honor of my noble Lord of York,   30
Dar'st thou maintain the former words thou spak'st?

BASSET
Yes, sir, as well as you dare patronage   32
The envious barking of your saucy tongue
Against my lord the Duke of Somerset.

VERNON
Sirrah, thy lord I honor as he is.

BASSET
Why, what is he? – as good a man as York.

VERNON
Hark ye, not so. In witness, take ye that.
  Vernon strikes him.

BASSET
Villain, thou know'st the law of arms is such
That whoso draws a sword 'tis present death,   39
Or else this blow should broach thy dearest blood.   40
But I'll unto his majesty and crave
I may have liberty to venge this wrong,   42
When thou shalt see I'll meet thee to thy cost.

---

23 *reguerdoned* rewarded   28 *hot* angry   29 *these colors* this badge (the rose)
32 *patronage* defend   39 *present* immediate (since dueling at court was pun-
ishable by death)   40 *broach* tap (as a vat of wine)   42 *liberty* permission

VERNON

44 Well, miscreant, I'll be there as soon as you,

45 And after meet you sooner than you would.   *Exeunt.*

*

∾ **IV.1** *Flourish. Enter King Henry, Humphrey Duke of*
Gloucester, the Bishop of Winchester, the Duke of
Exeter; Richard Duke of York, and the Earl of
Warwick with white roses; the Earl of Suffolk and
the Duke of Somerset with red roses; Lord Talbot,
and the Governor of Paris.

GLOUCESTER   *To Winchester*

Lord Bishop, set the crown upon his head.

BISHOP OF WINCHESTER

God save King Henry, of that name the sixth!
Winchester crowns the king.

GLOUCESTER

Now, Governor of Paris, take your oath

4 That you elect no other king but him;

Esteem none friends but such as are his friends,

6 And none your foes but such as shall pretend

Malicious practices against his state.

This shall ye do, so help you righteous God.
Enter Sir John Fastolf with a letter.

FASTOLF

My gracious sovereign, as I rode from Calais

10 To haste unto your coronation

A letter was delivered to my hands,
He presents the letter.

Writ to your grace from th' Duke of Burgundy.

TALBOT

Shame to the Duke of Burgundy and thee!

I vowed, base knight, when I did meet thee next,

---

44 *miscreant* villain 45 *would* would wish
IV.1 The palace, Paris 4 *elect* acknowledge 6 *pretend* intend

To tear the Garter from thy craven's leg,   15
   He tears it off.
Which I have done because unworthily
Thou wast installèd in that high degree. –
Pardon me, princely Henry and the rest.
This dastard at the battle of Patay   19
When but in all I was six thousand strong,   20
And that the French were almost ten to one,
Before we met, or that a stroke was given,
Like to a trusty squire did run away;   23
In which assault we lost twelve hundred men.
Myself and divers gentlemen beside
Were there surprised and taken prisoners.
Then judge, great lords, if I have done amiss,
Or whether that such cowards ought to wear
This ornament of knighthood: yea or no?

GLOUCESTER
To say the truth, this fact was infamous   30
And ill beseeming any common man,   31
Much more a knight, a captain and a leader.

TALBOT
When first this order was ordained, my lords,
Knights of the Garter were of noble birth,
Valiant and virtuous, full of haughty courage,   35
Such as were grown to credit by the wars;   36
Not fearing death nor shrinking for distress,   37
But always resolute in most extremes.   38
He then that is not furnished in this sort   39
Doth but usurp the sacred name of knight,   40
Profaning this most honorable order,
And should – if I were worthy to be judge –

---

15 *Garter* badge of the Order of the Garter; *craven's* coward's   19 *dastard* coward   20 *but in all* altogether   23 *trusty squire* (contemptuous)   30 *fact* misdeed   31 *common* lacking noble rank   35 *haughty* lofty   36 *were . . . credit* had risen to renown   37 *for distress* in face of hardship   38 *most* greatest   39 *furnished . . . sort* so endowed

43   Be quite degraded, like a hedge-born swain
44   That doth presume to boast of gentle blood.

KING HENRY   *To Fastolf*

45   Stain to thy countrymen, thou hear'st thy doom.
46   Be packing, therefore, thou that wast a knight.
    Henceforth we banish thee on pain of death.

Exit Fastolf.

    And now, my Lord Protector, view the letter
    Sent from our uncle, Duke of Burgundy.

GLOUCESTER

50   What means his grace that he hath changed his style?
    No more but plain and bluntly "To the king"?
    Hath he forgot he is his sovereign?
53   Or doth this churlish superscription
54   Pretend some alteration in good will?
    What's here? "I have upon especial cause,
56   Moved with compassion of my country's wrack
    Together with the pitiful complaints
    Of such as your oppression feeds upon,
    Forsaken your pernicious faction
60   And joined with Charles, the rightful King of France."
    O monstrous treachery! Can this be so?
    That in alliance, amity, and oaths
    There should be found such false dissembling guile?

KING HENRY

64   What? Doth my uncle Burgundy revolt?

GLOUCESTER

    He doth, my lord, and is become your foe.

KING HENRY

    Is that the worst this letter doth contain?

GLOUCESTER

    It is the worst, and all, my lord, he writes.

---

43 *degraded* reduced in rank; *hedge-born swain* lowborn rustic 44 *gentle* noble 45 *doom* sentence 46 *Be packing* be off 50 *style* form of address 53 *churlish superscription* rude address 54 *Pretend* indicate 56 *wrack* ruin 64 *uncle* (Henry's uncle the Duke of Bedford married Burgundy's sister Anne)

KING HENRY
 Why then, Lord Talbot there shall talk with him
 And give him chastisement for this abuse.
  To Talbot
 How say you, my lord? Are you not content?   *70*

TALBOT
 Content, my liege? Yes. But that I am prevented, *71*
 I should have begged I might have been employed.

KING HENRY
 Then gather strength and march unto him straight. *73*
 Let him perceive how ill we brook his treason,   *74*
 And what offense it is to flout his friends.

TALBOT
 I go, my lord, in heart desiring still   *76*
 You may behold confusion of your foes.   *Exit.*
  Enter Vernon wearing a white rose, and Basset
  wearing a red rose.

VERNON *To King Henry*
 Grant me the combat, gracious sovereign.   *78*

BASSET *To King Henry*
 And me, my lord; grant me the combat too.

RICHARD DUKE OF YORK
  To King Henry, pointing to Vernon
 This is my servant; hear him, noble prince.   *80*

SOMERSET *To King Henry, pointing to Basset*
 And this is mine, sweet Henry; favor him.

KING HENRY
 Be patient, lords, and give them leave to speak.
 Say, gentlemen, what makes you thus exclaim,
 And wherefore crave you combat, or with whom?

VERNON
 With him, my lord; for he hath done me wrong.

---

71 *am prevented* have been anticipated 73 *strength* forces; *straight* immediately 74 *brook* endure 76 *still* always 78 *the combat* a duel 80 *servant* retainer (not menial)

BASSET
    And I with him; for he hath done me wrong.

KING HENRY
    What is that wrong whereof you both complain?
    First let me know, and then I'll answer you.

BASSET
    Crossing the sea from England into France,
90   This fellow here with envious carping tongue
    Upbraided me about the rose I wear,
92   Saying the sanguine color of the leaves
    Did represent my master's blushing cheeks
94   When stubbornly he did repugn the truth
    About a certain question in the law
    Argued betwixt the Duke of York and him,
    With other vile and ignominious terms;
    In confutation of which rude reproach,
    And in defense of my lord's worthiness,
100   I crave the benefit of law of arms.

VERNON
    And that is my petition, noble lord;
102   For though he seem with forgèd quaint conceit
103   To set a gloss upon his bold intent,
    Yet know, my lord, I was provoked by him,
    And he first took exceptions at this badge,
    Pronouncing that the paleness of this flower
107   Bewrayed the faintness of my master's heart.

RICHARD DUKE OF YORK
108   Will not this malice, Somerset, be left?

SOMERSET
    Your private grudge, my Lord of York, will out,
110   Though ne'er so cunningly you smother it.

---

92 *sanguine* blood-red; *leaves* petals   94 *repugn* oppose   100 *benefit* legal privilege   102 *quaint conceit* ingenious fancy   103 *set . . . upon* give fair outward appearance to   107 *Bewrayed* revealed   108 *Will not . . . left* cannot . . . put to one side

KING HENRY
    Good Lord, what madness rules in brainsick men
    When for so slight and frivolous a cause
    Such factious emulations shall arise?   113
    Good cousins both of York and Somerset,
    Quiet yourselves, I pray, and be at peace.
RICHARD DUKE OF YORK
    Let this dissension first be tried by fight,
    And then your highness shall command a peace.
SOMERSET
    The quarrel toucheth none but us alone;   118
    Betwixt ourselves let us decide it then.
RICHARD DUKE OF YORK
    There is my pledge. Accept it, Somerset.   120
VERNON   *To King Henry*
    Nay, let it rest where it began at first.
BASSET   *To King Henry*
    Confirm it so, mine honorable lord.
GLOUCESTER
    Confirm it so? Confounded be your strife,
    And perish ye with your audacious prate!   124
    Presumptuous vassals, are you not ashamed
    With this immodest clamorous outrage
    To trouble and disturb the king and us?
    And you, my lords, methinks you do not well
    To bear with their perverse objections,   129
    Much less to take occasion from their mouths   130
    To raise a mutiny betwixt yourselves.
    Let me persuade you take a better course.
EXETER
    It grieves his highness. Good my lords, be friends.
KING HENRY
    Come hither, you that would be combatants.

---

113 *emulations* rivalries   118 *toucheth* involves   120 *pledge* gage in a duel
(usually a glove)   124 *prate* prattling   129 *objections* mutual accusations
130 *occasion* the opportunity

Henceforth I charge you, as you love our favor,
Quite to forget this quarrel and the cause.
And you, my lords, remember where we are –
In France, amongst a fickle wavering nation.
If they perceive dissension in our looks,
140   And that within ourselves we disagree,
141   How will their grudging stomachs be provoked
To willful disobedience, and rebel!
Beside, what infamy will there arise
144   When foreign princes shall be certified
145   That for a toy, a thing of no regard,
King Henry's peers and chief nobility
Destroyed themselves and lost the realm of France!
O, think upon the conquest of my father,
My tender years, and let us not forgo
150   That for a trifle that was bought with blood.
151   Let me be umpire in this doubtful strife.
I see no reason, if I wear this rose,
     He takes a red rose.
That anyone should therefore be suspicious
I more incline to Somerset than York.
Both are my kinsmen, and I love them both.
As well they may upbraid me with my crown
Because, forsooth, the King of Scots is crowned.
But your discretions better can persuade
Than I am able to instruct or teach,
160   And therefore, as we hither came in peace,
So let us still continue peace and love.
162   Cousin of York, we institute your grace
To be our regent in these parts of France;
And good my Lord of Somerset, unite
165   Your troops of horsemen with his bands of foot,
And like true subjects, sons of your progenitors,

---

141 *grudging stomachs* resentful tempers   144 *certified* informed   145 *toy*
trifle; *regard* consequence   150 *That . . . that* for a trifle that which   151
doubtful uncertain   162 *institute* appoint   165 *bands of foot* infantry

Go cheerfully together and digest   167
Your angry choler on your enemies.
Ourself, my Lord Protector, and the rest,
After some respite, will return to Calais,   170
From thence to England, where I hope ere long
To be presented by your victories
With Charles, Alençon, and that traitorous rout.   173

Flourish. Exeunt all but York, Warwick,
Vernon, and Exeter.

WARWICK
My Lord of York, I promise you, the king
Prettily, methought, did play the orator.

RICHARD DUKE OF YORK
And so he did; but yet I like it not
In that he wears the badge of Somerset.

WARWICK
Tush, that was but his fancy; blame him not.
I dare presume, sweet prince, he thought no harm.

RICHARD DUKE OF YORK
An if I wist he did – but let it rest.   180
Other affairs must now be managèd.

Exeunt all but Exeter.

EXETER
Well didst thou, Richard, to suppress thy voice;
For had the passions of thy heart burst out
I fear we should have seen deciphered there   184
More rancorous spite, more furious raging broils,
Than yet can be imagined or supposed.
But howsoe'er, no simple man that sees   187
This jarring discord of nobility,
This shouldering of each other in the court,
This factious bandying of their favorites,   190
But that it doth presage some ill event.   191

---

167 *digest* dissipate   173 *rout* rabble   180 *An . . . wist* if I knew for certain
184 *deciphered* revealed   187 *simple* common   190 *bandying* verbal quarreling; *favorites* followers   191 *But that* but sees that; *event* outcome

192 'Tis much when scepters are in children's hands,
193 But more when envy breeds unkind division:
       There comes the ruin, there begins confusion.   *Exit.*

                         *

∾ **IV.2** *Enter Lord Talbot with a Trumpeter and*
                  Drummer and Soldiers before Bordeaux.

TALBOT
     Go to the gates of Bordeaux, trumpeter.
     Summon their general unto the wall.
          The Trumpeter sounds a parley. Enter French General
          aloft.
     English John Talbot, captain, calls you forth,
     Servant in arms to Harry King of England;
5   And thus he would: open your city gates,
     Be humble to us, call my sovereign yours
     And do him homage as obedient subjects,
     And I'll withdraw me and my bloody power.
     But if you frown upon this proffered peace,
10   You tempt the fury of my three attendants –
11   Lean famine, quartering steel, and climbing fire –
12   Who in a moment even with the earth
13   Shall lay your stately and air-braving towers
     If you forsake the offer of their love.
FRENCH GENERAL
     Thou ominous and fearful owl of death,
     Our nation's terror and their bloody scourge,
17   The period of thy tyranny approacheth.
     On us thou canst not enter but by death,
     For I protest we are well fortified
20   And strong enough to issue out and fight.

———————

192 *much* serious   193 *unkind* unnatural (because intrafamily)
     IV.2 Before Bordeaux   5 *would* wishes   11 *quartering* dismembering the
slain enemy   12 *even* level   13 *air-braving* air-defying (because so lofty)
17 *period* end

If thou retire, the dauphin well appointed   21
Stands with the snares of war to tangle thee.
On either hand thee there are squadrons pitched   23
To wall thee from the liberty of flight,   24
And no way canst thou turn thee for redress
But death doth front thee with apparent spoil,   26
And pale destruction meets thee in the face.
Ten thousand French have ta'en the sacrament   28
To fire their dangerous artillery
Upon no Christian soul but English Talbot.   30
Lo, there thou stand'st, a breathing valiant man
Of an invincible unconquered spirit.
This is the latest glory of thy praise,   33
That I thy enemy due thee withal,   34
For ere the glass that now begins to run   35
Finish the process of his sandy hour,   36
These eyes that see thee now well colorèd   37
Shall see thee withered, bloody, pale, and dead.
    Drum afar off.
Hark, hark, the dauphin's drum, a warning bell,
Sings heavy music to thy timorous soul,   40
And mine shall ring thy dire departure out.   *Exit.*
TALBOT
He fables not. I hear the enemy.
Out, some light horsemen, and peruse their wings.   43
          Exit one or more.
O negligent and heedless discipline,   44
How are we parked and bounded in a pale! –   45
A little herd of England's timorous deer
Mazed with a yelping kennel of French curs.   47

---

21 *appointed* equipped   23 *thee* of thee; *pitched* set in battle order   24 *wall* hem in   26 *front* face; *spoil* slaughter (hunting metaphor, continued from *snares* in l. 22)   28 *ta'en the sacrament* i.e., sworn a solemn oath   33 *latest* final   34 *due* endow   35 *glass* hourglass   36 *process of his* progress of its   37 *well colorèd* in good health   43 *peruse their wings* survey their flanks   44 *heedless* careless   45 *parked* enclosed; *pale* fenced-in area   47 *Mazed* bewildered

48   If we be English deer, be then in blood,
49   Not rascal-like to fall down with a pinch,
50   But rather, moody-mad and desperate stags,
51   Turn on the bloody hounds with heads of steel
      And make the cowards stand aloof at bay.
      Sell every man his life as dear as mine
54   And they shall find dear deer of us, my friends.
      God and Saint George, Talbot and England's right,
      Prosper our colors in this dangerous fight!   *Exeunt.*

                         ✶

∾ **IV.3** *Enter a Messenger that meets the Duke of York.*
Enter Richard Duke of York with a Trumpeter and
many Soldiers.

RICHARD DUKE OF YORK
      Are not the speedy scouts returned again
2   That dogged the mighty army of the dauphin?
MESSENGER
3   They are returned, my lord, and give it out
      That he is marched to Bordeaux with his power
      To fight with Talbot. As he marched along,
6   By your espials were discoverèd
      Two mightier troops than that the dauphin led,
      Which joined with him and made their march for Bor-
          deaux.
RICHARD DUKE OF YORK
      A plague upon that villain Somerset
10   That thus delays my promisèd supply
      Of horsemen that were levièd for this siege!
      Renownèd Talbot doth expect my aid,
13   And I am louted by a traitor villain

---

48 *in blood* in prime vigor   **49** *rascal* (1) lean or inferior deer, (2) rabble;
pinch nip of the hounds   **50** *moody-mad* enraged   **51** *heads of steel* horns
like swords   **54** *dear* costly
   IV.3 A field somewhere in France   **2** *dogged* tracked   **3** *give it out* report
6 *espials* spies   **13** *louted* made a fool of

And cannot help the noble chevalier.
God comfort him in this necessity;
If he miscarry, farewell wars in France!   16
    Enter another Messenger, Sir William Lucy.

LUCY
Thou princely leader of our English strength,
Never so needful on the earth of France,
Spur to the rescue of the noble Talbot,
Who now is girdled with a waste of iron   20
And hemmed about with grim destruction.
To Bordeaux, warlike duke; to Bordeaux, York,
Else farewell Talbot, France, and England's honor.

RICHARD DUKE OF YORK
O God, that Somerset, who in proud heart
Doth stop my cornets, were in Talbot's place!   25
So should we save a valiant gentleman
By forfeiting a traitor and a coward.
Mad ire and wrathful fury makes me weep,
That thus we die while remiss traitors sleep.   29

LUCY
O, send some succor to the distressed lord.   30

RICHARD DUKE OF YORK
He dies, we lose; I break my warlike word;
We mourn, France smiles; we lose, they daily get,
All 'long of this vile traitor Somerset.   33

LUCY
Then God take mercy on brave Talbot's soul,
And on his son young John, who two hours since
I met in travel toward his warlike father.
This seven years did not Talbot see his son,
And now they meet where both their lives are done.

RICHARD DUKE OF YORK
Alas, what joy shall noble Talbot have

---

16 *miscarry* come to harm 20 *waste* (1) vast expanse, (2) belt 25 *cornets*
companies of cavalry 29 *remiss* (1) idle, (2) negligent 30 *distressed* in diffi-
culties (not "upset") 33 *'long* because

40   To bid his young son welcome to his grave?
      Away – vexation almost stops my breath
      That sundered friends greet in the hour of death.
43   Lucy, farewell. No more my fortune can
      But curse the cause I cannot aid the man.
      Maine, Blois, Poitiers, and Tours are won away
46   'Long all of Somerset and his delay.

Exeunt all but Lucy.

LUCY
      Thus while the vulture of sedition
      Feeds in the bosom of such great commanders,
49   Sleeping neglection doth betray to loss
50   The conquest of our scarce-cold conqueror,
51   That ever-living man of memory
      Henry the Fifth. Whiles they each other cross,
      Lives, honors, lands, and all hurry to loss.   *Exit.*

*

❧ **IV.4** *Enter the Duke of Somerset with his Army.*

SOMERSET   *To a Captain*
      It is too late, I cannot send them now.
      This expedition was by York and Talbot
3   Too rashly plotted. All our general force
      Might with a sally of the very town
      Be buckled with. The overdaring Talbot
      Hath sullied all his gloss of former honor
      By this unheedful, desperate, wild adventure.
      York set him on to fight and die in shame
9   That, Talbot dead, great York might bear the name.
      Enter Sir William Lucy.

------

43 *can* is able to do **46** *'Long all* all because **49** *Sleeping neglection* careless disregard **51** *ever-living . . . memory* man of ever-living memory
    IV.4 A field in France **3–5** *All . . . with* the mere town garrison, without other aid, might safely come forth to engage our whole army **9** *bear the name* claim preeminence

CAPTAIN
  Here is Sir William Lucy, who with me   *10*
  Set from our o'ermatched forces forth for aid.
SOMERSET
  How now, Sir William, whither were you sent?
LUCY
  Whither, my lord? From bought and sold Lord Talbot,   *13*
  Who, ringed about with bold adversity,
  Cries out for noble York and Somerset
  To beat assailing death from his weak legions;
  And whiles the honorable captain there
  Drops bloody sweat from his war-wearied limbs
  And, unadvantaged, ling'ring looks for rescue,   *19*
  You his false hopes, the trust of England's honor,   *20*
  Keep off aloof with worthless emulation.   *21*
  Let not your private discord keep away
  The levied succors that should lend him aid,   *23*
  While he, renownèd noble gentleman,
  Yield up his life unto a world of odds.   *25*
  Orléans the Bastard, Charles, and Burgundy,
  Alençon, René compass him about,
  And Talbot perisheth by your default.
SOMERSET
  York set him on; York should have sent him aid.
LUCY
  And York as fast upon your grace exclaims,   *30*
  Swearing that you withhold his levied horse
  Collected for this expedition.
SOMERSET
  York lies. He might have sent and had the horse.   *33*
  I owe him little duty and less love,

---

13 *bought and sold* i.e., betrayed as by Judas   **19** *unadvantaged* disadvantaged   **20** *trust* trustee   **21** *worthless emulation* senseless rivalry   **23** *succors* reinforcements   **25** *a world of* immense   **30** *upon . . . exclaims* accuses your grace   **33** *sent* sent for

35   And take foul scorn to fawn on him by sending.

LUCY
           The fraud of England, not the force of France,
           Hath now entrapped the noble-minded Talbot.
           Never to England shall he bear his life,
           But dies betrayed to fortune by your strife.

SOMERSET
40   Come, go. I will dispatch the horsemen straight.
           Within six hours they will be at his aid.

LUCY
           Too late comes rescue. He is ta'en or slain,
           For fly he could not if he would have fled,
           And fly would Talbot never, though he might.

SOMERSET
           If he be dead, brave Talbot, then adieu.

LUCY
           His fame lives in the world, his shame in you.
                                        Exeunt severally.

                              *

∽ **IV.5** *Enter Lord Talbot and his son John.*

TALBOT
           O young John Talbot, I did send for thee
           To tutor thee in stratagems of war,
           That Talbot's name might be in thee revived
4   When sapless age and weak unable limbs
           Should bring thy father to his drooping chair.
           But O – malignant and ill-boding stars! –
           Now thou art come unto a feast of death,
8   A terrible and unavoided danger.
           Therefore, dear boy, mount on my swiftest horse,
10   And I'll direct thee how thou shalt escape

---

35 *take . . . scorn* find it disgraceful
   IV.5 Battlefield near Bordeaux   4 *sapless* withered   8 *unavoided* unavoidable

By sudden flight. Come, dally not, be gone.

YOUNG TALBOT
Is my name Talbot, and am I your son,
And shall I fly? O, if you love my mother,
Dishonor not her honorable name
To make a bastard and a slave of me.
The world will say he is not Talbot's blood
That basely fled when noble Talbot stood.

TALBOT
Fly to revenge my death if I be slain.

YOUNG TALBOT
He that flies so will ne'er return again.

TALBOT
If we both stay, we both are sure to die.   20

YOUNG TALBOT
Then let me stay and, father, do you fly.
Your loss is great; so your regard should be.   22
My worth unknown, no loss is known in me.
Upon my death the French can little boast;
In yours they will: in you all hopes are lost.
Flight cannot stain the honor you have won,
But mine it will, that no exploit have done.
You fled for vantage, every one will swear,   28
But if I bow, they'll say it was for fear.
There is no hope that ever I will stay   30
If the first hour I shrink and run away.
Here on my knee I beg mortality   32
Rather than life preserved with infamy.

TALBOT
Shall all thy mother's hopes lie in one tomb?

YOUNG TALBOT
Ay, rather than I'll shame my mother's womb.

---

22 *regard* concern for yourself   28 *vantage* military advantage   **32** *mortality*
death

TALBOT
> Upon my blessing I command thee go.

YOUNG TALBOT
> To fight I will, but not to fly the foe.

TALBOT
> Part of thy father may be saved in thee.

YOUNG TALBOT
> No part of him but will be shamed in me.

TALBOT
40   Thou never hadst renown, nor canst not lose it.

YOUNG TALBOT
> Yes, your renownèd name – shall flight abuse it?

TALBOT
42   Thy father's charge shall clear thee from that stain.

YOUNG TALBOT
43   You cannot witness for me, being slain.
44   If death be so apparent, then both fly.

TALBOT
> And leave my followers here to fight and die?
46   My age was never tainted with such shame.

YOUNG TALBOT
> And shall my youth be guilty of such blame?
> No more can I be severed from your side
> Than can yourself your self in twain divide.
50   Stay, go, do what you will: the like do I,
> For live I will not if my father die.

TALBOT
> Then here I take my leave of thee, fair son,
53   Born to eclipse thy life this afternoon.
> Come, side by side together live and die,
> And soul with soul from France to heaven fly.   *Exeunt.*

*

---

42 *charge* order   43 *being slain* if you are slain   44 *apparent* certain   46 *age* lifetime   53 *eclipse* extinguish

∾ **IV.6** *Alarum. Excursions, wherein Lord Talbot's son*
   John is hemmed about by French Soldiers and Talbot
   rescues him. The English drive off the French.

TALBOT
   Saint George and victory! Fight, soldiers, fight!
   The regent hath with Talbot broke his word,
   And left us to the rage of France his sword.   3
   Where is John Talbot? *(To John)* Pause and take thy
      breath.
   I gave thee life, and rescued thee from death.
YOUNG TALBOT
   O twice my father, twice am I thy son:
   The life thou gav'st me first was lost and done
   Till with thy warlike sword, despite of fate,
   To my determined time thou gav'st new date.   9
TALBOT
   When from the dauphin's crest thy sword struck fire   10
   It warmed thy father's heart with proud desire
   Of bold-faced victory. Then leaden age,
   Quickened with youthful spleen and warlike rage,   13
   Beat down Alençon, Orléans, Burgundy,
   And from the pride of Gallia rescued thee.   15
   The ireful Bastard Orléans, that drew blood
   From thee, my boy, and had the maidenhood
   Of thy first fight, I soon encounterèd,
   And interchanging blows, I quickly shed
   Some of his bastard blood, and in disgrace   20
   Bespoke him thus: "Contaminated, base,
   And misbegotten blood I spill of thine,
   Mean and right poor, for that pure blood of mine   23
   Which thou didst force from Talbot, my brave boy."

IV.6 Battlefield near Bordeaux   **3** *France his* France's   **9** *determined* exactly
defined; *date* limit   **13** *Quickened* revived; *spleen* courage   **15** *Gallia* France
20 *in disgrace* as an insult   **23** *Mean* inferior

25   Here, purposing the Bastard to destroy,
Came in strong rescue. Speak thy father's care:
Art thou not weary, John? How dost thou fare?
Wilt thou yet leave the battle, boy, and fly,

29   Now thou art sealed the son of chivalry?

30   Fly to revenge my death when I am dead;

31   The help of one stands me in little stead.

32   O, too much folly is it, well I wot,
To hazard all our lives in one small boat.
If I today die not with Frenchmen's rage,

35   Tomorrow I shall die with mickle age.
By me they nothing gain, and if I stay
'Tis but the short'ning of my life one day.
In thee thy mother dies, our household's name,
My death's revenge, thy youth, and England's fame.

40   All these and more we hazard by thy stay;
All these are saved if thou wilt fly away.

YOUNG TALBOT

42   The sword of Orléans hath not made me smart;
These words of yours draw lifeblood from my heart.

44   On that advantage, bought with such a shame,
To save a paltry life and slay bright fame,
Before young Talbot from old Talbot fly

47   The coward horse that bears me fall and die;

48   And like me to the peasant boys of France,
To be shame's scorn and subject of mischance!

50   Surely, by all the glory you have won,
An if I fly I am not Talbot's son.

52   Then talk no more of flight; it is no boot.
If son to Talbot, die at Talbot's foot.

TALBOT

54   Then follow thou thy desp'rate sire of Crete,

---

25 *purposing* as I purposed   29 *sealed* certified   31 *stands . . . stead* does me little good   32 *wot* knew   35 *mickle* great   42 *smart* suffer   44 *On that advantage* to gain these benefits (i.e., safety, revenge)   47 *fall* may it fall   48 *like* liken   52 *boot* use   54 *Crete* the site of the labyrinth from which Daedalus and his son *Icarus* attempted to escape on wings

Thou Icarus; thy life to me is sweet.
If thou wilt fight, fight by thy father's side,
And commendable proved, let's die in pride.   *Exeunt.*

✻

✆ **IV.7** *Alarum. Excursions. Enter old Lord Talbot, led
by a Servant.*

TALBOT
Where is my other life? Mine own is gone.
O where's young Talbot, where is valiant John?
Triumphant death smeared with captivity,   3
Young Talbot's valor makes me smile at thee.
When he perceived me shrink and on my knee,   5
His bloody sword he brandished over me,
And like a hungry lion did commence
Rough deeds of rage and stern impatience.
But when my angry guardant stood alone,   9
Tend'ring my ruin and assailed of none,   10
Dizzy-eyed fury and great rage of heart
Suddenly made him from my side to start
Into the clust'ring battle of the French,   13
And in that sea of blood my boy did drench   14
His overmounting spirit; and there died
My Icarus, my blossom, in his pride.
    Enter English Soldiers with John Talbot's body, borne.
SERVANT
O my dear lord, lo where your son is borne.
TALBOT
Thou antic death, which laugh'st us here to scorn,   18
Anon from thy insulting tyranny,   19
Coupled in bonds of perpetuity,   20

IV.7 *Battlefield near Bordeaux* **3** *captivity* the blood of captives **5** *shrink*
give way in battle **9** *guardant* protector **10** *Tend'ring* concerned for **13**
clust'ring battle swarming army **14** *drench* drown **18** *antic* grotesquely
grinning (like a skull) **19** *Anon* soon

21 Two Talbots wingèd through the lither sky
In thy despite shall scape mortality.
    To Young Talbot
23 O thou whose wounds become hard-favored death,
Speak to thy father ere thou yield thy breath.
25 Brave death by speaking, whether he will or no;
Imagine him a Frenchman and thy foe. –
27 Poor boy, he smiles, methinks, as who should say
"Had death been French, then death had died today."
Come, come, and lay him in his father's arms.
    Soldiers lay Young Talbot in Talbot's arms.
30 My spirit can no longer bear these harms.
Soldiers, adieu. I have what I would have,
Now my old arms are young John Talbot's grave.
    He dies. Alarum. Exeunt Soldiers, leaving the bodies.
    Enter Charles the Dauphin, the Dukes of Alençon and
    Burgundy, the Bastard of Orléans, and Joan la Pucelle.

CHARLES
Had York and Somerset brought rescue in,
We should have found a bloody day of this.

BASTARD
35 How the young whelp of Talbot's, raging wood,
36 Did flesh his puny sword in Frenchmen's blood!

JOAN
Once I encountered him, and thus I said:
38 "Thou maiden youth, be vanquished by a maid."
But with a proud, majestical high scorn
40 He answered thus: "Young Talbot was not born
41 To be the pillage of a giglot wench."
42 So rushing in the bowels of the French,
He left me proudly, as unworthy fight.

---

21 *lither* yielding 23 *become . . . death* make beautiful even the hideous visage of death 25 *Brave* defy 27 *as who* as if one 35 *wood* mad 36 *puny* used for the first time in battle 38 *maiden* untried in battle 41 *pillage* plunder; *giglot* wanton 42 *bowels* center

BURGUNDY

   Doubtless he would have made a noble knight.

   See where he lies inhearsèd in the arms   45

   Of the most bloody nurser of his harms.   46

BASTARD

   Hew them to pieces, hack their bones asunder,

   Whose life was England's glory, Gallia's wonder.   48

CHARLES

   O no, forbear; for that which we have fled

   During the life, let us not wrong it dead.   *50*

     Enter Sir William Lucy with a French Herald.

LUCY

   Herald, conduct me to the dauphin's tent

   To know who hath obtained the glory of the day.

CHARLES

   On what submissive message art thou sent?

LUCY

   Submission, dauphin? 'Tis a mere French word.   54

   We English warriors wot not what it means.   55

   I come to know what prisoners thou hast ta'en,

   And to survey the bodies of the dead.

CHARLES

   For prisoners ask'st thou? Hell our prison is.   58

   But tell me whom thou seek'st.

LUCY

   But where's the great Alcides of the field,   60

   Valiant Lord Talbot, Earl of Shrewsbury,

   Created for his rare success in arms

   Great Earl of Wexford, Waterford, and Valence,

   Lord Talbot of Goodrich and Urchinfield,

   Lord Strange of Blackmere, Lord Verdun of Alton,

---

45 *inhearsèd* as in a coffin   46 *nurser . . . harms* one who fostered his injurious power (toward the French)   48 *Gallia's* France's   54 *mere* purely   55 *wot* know   58 *Hell . . . is* i.e., we dispatch our victims straight to hell   60 *Alcides* Hercules, son of Alcaeus

    Lord Cromwell of Wingfield, Lord Furnival of Shef-
      field,
    The thrice victorious Lord of Falconbridge,
    Knight of the noble order of Saint George,
69   Worthy Saint Michael and the Golden Fleece,
70   Great *Maréchal* to Henry the Sixth
    Of all his wars within the realm of France?

JOAN

72   Here's a silly, stately style indeed.
73   The Turk, that two and fifty kingdoms hath,
    Writes not so tedious a style as this.
    Him that thou magnifi'st with all these titles
76   Stinking and flyblown lies here at our feet.

LUCY

    Is Talbot slain, the Frenchmen's only scourge,
78   Your kingdom's terror and black Nemesis?
    O, were mine eyeballs into bullets turned,
80   That I in rage might shoot them at your faces!
    O, that I could but call these dead to life! –
    It were enough to fright the realm of France.
    Were but his picture left amongst you here
84   It would amaze the proudest of you all.
    Give me their bodies, that I may bear them hence
86   And give them burial as beseems their worth.

JOAN   *To Charles*

    I think this upstart is old Talbot's ghost,
    He speaks with such a proud commanding spirit.
    For God's sake let him have them. To keep them here
90   They would but stink and putrefy the air.

CHARLES

    Go, take their bodies hence.

---

69 *Worthy* worthy of   70 *Maréchal* commander in chief   72 *style* list of titles
73 *Turk* sultan of Turkey   76 *flyblown* putrefied   78 *Nemesis* goddess of
retributive justice   84 *amaze* terrify   86 *as beseems* as is appropriate to

LUCY
    I'll bear them hence, but from their ashes shall be
      reared
    A phoenix that shall make all France afeard.   *93*
CHARLES
    So we be rid of them, do with them what thou wilt.
                Exeunt Lucy and Herald with the bodies.
    And now to Paris in this conquering vein.
    All will be ours, now bloody Talbot's slain.   *Exeunt.*

                      *

∾ **V.1** *Sennet. Enter King Henry, the Dukes of*
    Gloucester and Exeter, and others.

KING HENRY   *To Gloucester*
    Have you perused the letters from the pope,
    The emperor, and the Earl of Armagnac?
GLOUCESTER
    I have, my lord, and their intent is this:
    They humbly sue unto your excellence
    To have a godly peace concluded of
    Between the realms of England and of France.
KING HENRY
    How doth your grace affect their motion?   *7*
GLOUCESTER
    Well, my good lord, and as the only means
    To stop effusion of our Christian blood   *9*
    And 'stablish quietness on every side.   *10*
KING HENRY
    Ay, marry, uncle; for I always thought
    It was both impious and unnatural
    That such immanity and bloody strife   *13*

---

93 *phoenix* mythical bird that arises regenerated from its own ashes
   V.1 The palace, London   **7** *affect* incline toward; *motion* proposal   **9** *ef-*
fusion spilling   **13** *immanity* monstrous cruelty

Should reign among professors of one faith.

GLOUCESTER

Beside, my lord, the sooner to effect

And surer bind this knot of amity,

17 The Earl of Armagnac, near knit to Charles –

A man of great authority in France –

Proffers his only daughter to your grace

20 In marriage, with a large and sumptuous dowry.

KING HENRY

Marriage, uncle? Alas, my years are young,

And fitter is my study and my books

Than wanton dalliance with a paramour.

Yet call th' ambassadors,　　　　*(Exit one or more.)*

　　　　　　　　　and as you please,

So let them have their answers every one.

I shall be well content with any choice

27 Tends to God's glory and my country's weal.

　　Enter Winchester, now in cardinal's habit, and three
　　Ambassadors, one a Papal Legate.

EXETER　*Aside*

What, is my Lord of Winchester installed

And called unto a cardinal's degree?

30 Then I perceive that will be verified

31 Henry the Fifth did sometime prophesy:

"If once he come to be a cardinal,

33 He'll make his cap coequal with the crown."

KING HENRY

My lords ambassadors, your several suits

Have been considered and debated on.

Your purpose is both good and reasonable,

And therefore are we certainly resolved

38 To draw conditions of a friendly peace,

Which by my Lord of Winchester we mean

---

17 *knit* related　27 *Tends* which tends; *weal* welfare　31 *sometime* at one time　33 *cap* cardinal's red hat　38 *draw* draft

Shall be transported presently to France.   40

GLOUCESTER   *To the Ambassadors*
And for the proffer of my lord your master,
I have informed his highness so at large   42
As, liking of the lady's virtuous gifts,   43
Her beauty, and the value of her dower,
He doth intend she shall be England's queen.

KING HENRY   *To the Ambassadors*
In argument and proof of which contract   46
Bear her this jewel, pledge of my affection.
      To Gloucester
And so, my Lord Protector, see them guarded
And safely brought to Dover, wherein shipped,   49
Commit them to the fortune of the sea.   50
          Exeunt severally all but Winchester and Legate.

CARDINAL OF WINCHESTER
Stay, my Lord Legate; you shall first receive
The sum of money which I promisèd
Should be delivered to his holiness
For clothing me in these grave ornaments.   54

LEGATE
I will attend upon your lordship's leisure.   *Exit.*

CARDINAL OF WINCHESTER
Now Winchester will not submit, I trow,   56
Or be inferior to the proudest peer.
Humphrey of Gloucester, thou shalt well perceive
That nor in birth or for authority   59
The bishop will be overborne by thee.   60
I'll either make thee stoop and bend thy knee,
Or sack this country with a mutiny.   *Exit.*   62

                              *

---

40 *presently* immediately   **42** *at large* fully   **43** *As, liking of* that, he so likes
46 *argument* support   **49** *wherein shipped* where once embarked   **54** *grave
ornaments* solemn robes of office   **56** *trow* trust   **59** *nor* neither   **60** *overborne* overruled   **62** *a mutiny* an open revolt

❧ **V.2** *Enter Charles the Dauphin reading a letter,
the Dukes of Burgundy and Alençon, the Bastard
of Orléans, René Duke of Anjou, and Joan la Pucelle.*

CHARLES
    These news, my lords, may cheer our drooping spirits.
2   'Tis said the stout Parisians do revolt
    And turn again unto the warlike French.
ALENÇON
    Then march to Paris, royal Charles of France,
5   And keep not back your powers in dalliance.
JOAN
    Peace be amongst them if they turn to us;
7   Else, ruin combat with their palaces!
        Enter a Scout.
SCOUT
    Success unto our valiant general,
9   And happiness to his accomplices.
CHARLES
10 What tidings send our scouts? I prithee speak.
SCOUT
    The English army, that divided was
    Into two parties, is now conjoined in one,
    And means to give you battle presently.
CHARLES
    Somewhat too sudden, sirs, the warning is;
    But we will presently provide for them.
BURGUNDY
    I trust the ghost of Talbot is not there.
JOAN
    Now he is gone, my lord, you need not fear.
    Of all base passions, fear is most accursed.
    Command the conquest, Charles, it shall be thine;

V.2 Plains in Anjou, France   **2** *stout* brave   **5** *dalliance* idleness   **7** *Else . . .
palaces* otherwise let ruin destroy their palaces   **9** *accomplices* allies

Let Henry fret and all the world repine.   20
CHARLES
Then on, my lords; and France be fortunate!   *Exeunt.*

*

∾ **V.3** *Alarum. Excursions. Enter Joan la Pucelle.*

JOAN
The regent conquers, and the Frenchmen fly.   1
Now help, ye charming spells and periapts,   2
And ye choice spirits that admonish me   3
And give me signs of future accidents.   4
     Thunder.
You speedy helpers, that are substitutes   5
Under the lordly monarch of the north,
Appear, and aid me in this enterprise.
     Enter Fiends.
This speed and quick appearance argues proof   8
Of your accustomed diligence to me.   9
Now, ye familiar spirits that are culled   10
Out of the powerful regions under earth,
Help me this once, that France may get the field.   12
     They walk and speak not.
O, hold me not with silence overlong!
Where I was wont to feed you with my blood,   14
I'll lop a member off and give it you   15
In earnest of a further benefit,   16
So you do condescend to help me now.
     They hang their heads.
No hope to have redress? My body shall

---

20 *repine* complain
   V.3 Before Angiers, France **1** *regent* i.e., Richard, Duke of York **2**
charming magic; *periapts* amulets **3** *admonish* forewarn **4** *accidents* events
5 *substitutes* deputies **8** *argues* offers **9** *accustomed* customary **12** *get the
field* win the battle **14** *feed . . . blood* (witches were thought to have an extra
nipple from which their attendant spirits would feed) **15** *member* limb **16**
In earnest as a down payment

Pay recompense if you will grant my suit.
   They shake their heads.
20 Cannot my body nor blood sacrifice
21 Entreat you to your wonted furtherance?
    Then take my soul – my body, soul, and all –
23 Before that England give the French the foil.
                           They depart.
    See, they forsake me. Now the time is come
25 That France must vail her lofty-plumèd crest
    And let her head fall into England's lap.
27 My ancient incantations are too weak,
28 And hell too strong for me to buckle with.
    Now, France, thy glory droopeth to the dust.   *Exit.*

                          *

∞ **V.4** *Excursions. The Dukes of Burgundy and York*
      fight hand to hand. The French fly. Joan la Pucelle
      is taken.

RICHARD DUKE OF YORK
    Damsel of France, I think I have you fast.
2 Unchain your spirits now with spelling charms,
    And try if they can gain your liberty.
    A goodly prize, fit for the devil's grace!
      To his Soldiers
5 See how the ugly witch doth bend her brows,
6 As if with Circe she would change my shape.
JOAN
    Changed to a worser shape thou canst not be.
RICHARD DUKE OF YORK
8 O, Charles the Dauphin is a proper man.
9 No shape but his can please your dainty eye.

---

21 *wonted furtherance* usual assistance **23** *foil* defeat **25** *vail* lower **27**
ancient former **28** *buckle* fight
    V.4 Before Angiers **2** *spelling charms* charms that cast spells **5** *doth
bend her brows* scowls **6** *Circe* a fabled sorceress who turned men into swine
8 *proper* handsome **9** *dainty* fastidious

JOAN
  A plaguing mischief light on Charles and thee,   10
  And may ye both be suddenly surprised   11
  By bloody hands in sleeping on your beds!   12
RICHARD DUKE OF YORK
  Fell banning hag, enchantress, hold thy tongue.   13
JOAN
  I prithee give me leave to curse awhile.
RICHARD DUKE OF YORK
  Curse, miscreant, when thou comest to the stake.   15
                                        Exeunt.

                          *

∾ **V.5** *Alarum. Enter the Earl of Suffolk with Margaret*
    in his hand.

SUFFOLK
  Be what thou wilt, thou art my prisoner.
      He gazes on her.
  O fairest beauty, do not fear nor fly,
  For I will touch thee but with reverent hands,
  And lay them gently on thy tender side.
  I kiss these fingers for eternal peace.   5
  Who art thou? Say, that I may honor thee.
MARGARET
  Margaret my name, and daughter to a king,
  The King of Naples, whosoe'er thou art.
SUFFOLK
  An earl I am, and Suffolk am I called.
  Be not offended, nature's miracle,   10
  Thou art allotted to be ta'en by me.   11
  So doth the swan his downy cygnets save,   12

  _____

  11 *surprised* captured **12** *in* while **13** *Fell banning* fierce cursing **15** *miscreant* heretic
      V.5 Before Angiers **s.d.** *in his* led by the **5** *for* in token of **11** *allotted*
  destined **12** *cygnets save* young swans protect

Keeping them prisoner underneath his wings.
14   Yet if this servile usage once offend,
Go, and be free again, as Suffolk's friend.
          She is going.
O stay! *(Aside)* I have no power to let her pass.
My hand would free her, but my heart says no.
18   As plays the sun upon the glassy stream,
Twinkling another counterfeited beam,
20   So seems this gorgeous beauty to mine eyes.
Fain would I woo her, yet I dare not speak.
I'll call for pen and ink, and write my mind.
23   Fie, de la Pole, disable not thyself!
Hast not a tongue? Is she not here to hear?
Wilt thou be daunted at a woman's sight?
Ay, beauty's princely majesty is such
27   Confounds the tongue, and makes the senses rough.

MARGARET
Say, Earl of Suffolk – if thy name be so –
What ransom must I pay before I pass?
30   For I perceive I am thy prisoner.

SUFFOLK   *Aside*
31   How canst thou tell she will deny thy suit
Before thou make a trial of her love?

MARGARET
Why speak'st thou not? What ransom must I pay?

SUFFOLK   *Aside*
She's beautiful, and therefore to be wooed;
She is a woman, therefore to be won.

MARGARET
Wilt thou accept of ransom, yea or no?

SUFFOLK   *Aside*
37   Fond man, remember that thou hast a wife;

---

14 *servile usage* slavelike treatment   18–20 *As plays . . . eyes* i.e., she seems as
gorgeous as the sun's reflection twinkling upon the water's surface   23 *disable* disparage   27 *Confounds* that it confuses; *rough* dull   31 *deny* refuse
37 *Fond* foolish

Then how can Margaret be thy paramour?   38
MARGARET   *Aside*
I were best to leave him, for he will not hear.
SUFFOLK   *Aside*
There all is marred; there lies a cooling card.   40
MARGARET   *Aside*
He talks at random; sure the man is mad.
SUFFOLK   *Aside*
And yet a dispensation may be had.
MARGARET
And yet I would that you would answer me.
SUFFOLK   *Aside*
I'll win this Lady Margaret. For whom?
Why, for my king – tush, that's a wooden thing.   45
MARGARET   *Aside*
He talks of wood. It is some carpenter.
SUFFOLK   *Aside*
Yet so my fancy may be satisfied,   47
And peace establishèd between these realms.
But there remains a scruple in that too,   49
For though her father be the King of Naples,   50
Duke of Anjou and Maine, yet is he poor,
And our nobility will scorn the match.
MARGARET
Hear ye, captain? Are you not at leisure?
SUFFOLK   *Aside*
It shall be so, disdain they ne'er so much.
Henry is youthful, and will quickly yield.
    To Margaret
Madam, I have a secret to reveal.
MARGARET   *Aside*
What though I be enthralled, he seems a knight   57
And will not any way dishonor me.

---

38 *paramour* mistress   40 *There* by that fact; *a cooling card* an opponent's
card that dashes one's hopes   45 *wooden* stupid (either the king or the plan
itself)   47 *fancy* desire   49 *scruple* objection   57 *enthralled* captive

SUFFOLK

59   Lady, vouchsafe to listen what I say.

MARGARET   *Aside*

60   Perhaps I shall be rescued by the French,
And then I need not crave his courtesy.

SUFFOLK

Sweet madam, give me hearing in a cause.

MARGARET   *Aside*

Tush, women have been captivate ere now.

SUFFOLK

Lady, wherefore talk you so?

MARGARET

65   I cry you mercy, 'tis but *quid* for *quo*.

SUFFOLK

Say, gentle princess, would you not suppose

67   Your bondage happy to be made a queen?

MARGARET

To be a queen in bondage is more vile

69   Than is a slave in base servility,

70   For princes should be free.

SUFFOLK   And so shall you,
If happy England's royal king be free.

MARGARET

Why, what concerns his freedom unto me?

SUFFOLK

I'll undertake to make thee Henry's queen,
To put a golden scepter in thy hand,
And set a precious crown upon thy head,

76   If thou wilt condescend to be my –

MARGARET   What?

SUFFOLK

His love.

MARGARET

I am unworthy to be Henry's wife.

---

59 *listen* listen to   65 *cry you mercy* beg your pardon; *quid for quo* tit for tat
67 *to be* if you were to be   69 *servility* slavery   76 *condescend* agree

SUFFOLK
  No, gentle madam, I unworthy am
  To woo so fair a dame to be his wife   *80*
    Aside
  And have no portion in the choice myself.   *81*
    To Margaret
  How say you, madam; are ye so content?
MARGARET
  An if my father please, I am content.
SUFFOLK
  Then call our captains and our colors forth,
    Enter Captains, Colors, and Trumpeters.
  And, madam, at your father's castle walls
  We'll crave a parley to confer with him.
    Sound a parley. Enter René Duke of Anjou
    on the walls.
  See, René, see thy daughter prisoner.
RENÉ
  To whom?
SUFFOLK   To me.
RENÉ   Suffolk, what remedy?
  I am a soldier, and unapt to weep   *89*
  Or to exclaim on fortune's fickleness.   *90*
SUFFOLK
  Yes, there is remedy enough, my lord.
  Assent, and for thy honor give consent
  Thy daughter shall be wedded to my king,
  Whom I with pain have wooed and won thereto;
  And this her easy-held imprisonment   *95*
  Hath gained thy daughter princely liberty.
RENÉ
  Speaks Suffolk as he thinks?
SUFFOLK   Fair Margaret knows

---

81 *portion* share; *the choice* (1) the choosing, (2) the thing chosen   **89** *unapt*
unsuited   **90** *exclaim on* complain of   **95** *easy-held* easily endured

98   That Suffolk doth not flatter, face or feign.

RENÉ

99   Upon thy princely warrant I descend
100   To give thee answer of thy just demand.

SUFFOLK

101   And here I will expect thy coming.   *Exit René above.*
          Trumpets sound. Enter René.

RENÉ

      Welcome, brave earl, into our territories.
      Command in Anjou what your honor pleases.

SUFFOLK

104   Thanks, René, happy for so sweet a child,
      Fit to be made companion with a king.
      What answer makes your grace unto my suit?

RENÉ

      Since thou dost deign to woo her little worth
      To be the princely bride of such a lord,
      Upon condition I may quietly
110   Enjoy mine own, the countries Maine and Anjou,
      Free from oppression or the stroke of war,
      My daughter shall be Henry's, if he please.

SUFFOLK

      That is her ransom. I deliver her,
114   And those two counties I will undertake
      Your grace shall well and quietly enjoy.

RENÉ

116   And I again in Henry's royal name,
117   As deputy unto that gracious king,
118   Give thee her hand for sign of plighted faith.

SUFFOLK

      René of France, I give thee kingly thanks,
120   Because this is in traffic of a king.

---

98 *face* deceive   99 *warrant* guarantee   101 *expect* await   104 *happy for* fortunate in having   114 *counties* domains of a count   116 *again* in return   117 *deputy* (refers to Suffolk)   118 *plighted faith* a marriage pledge   120 *traffic* business

Aside
And yet methinks I could be well content
To be mine own attorney in this case.
   To René
I'll over then to England with this news,
And make this marriage to be solemnized.
So farewell, René; set this diamond safe
In golden palaces, as it becomes.   126

RENÉ
I do embrace thee as I would embrace
The Christian prince King Henry, were he here.

MARGARET   *To Suffolk*
Farewell, my lord. Good wishes, praise, and prayers
Shall Suffolk ever have of Margaret.   130
   She is going.

SUFFOLK
Farewell, sweet madam; but hark you, Margaret –
No princely commendations to my king?   132

MARGARET
Such commendations as becomes a maid,
A virgin, and his servant, say to him.

SUFFOLK
Words sweetly placed, and modestly directed.
   She is going.
But madam, I must trouble you again –
No loving token to his majesty?

MARGARET
Yes, my good lord: a pure unspotted heart,
Never yet taint with love, I send the king.   139

SUFFOLK
And this withal.   140
   He kisses her.

MARGARET
That for thyself; I will not so presume

---

126 *as it becomes* as befits (such a jewel)   132 *commendations* greetings   **139**
taint tainted   140 *withal* moreover

142   To send such peevish tokens to a king.

                                      Exeunt René and Margaret.

SUFFOLK   *Aside*

    O, wert thou for myself! – but Suffolk, stay.

    Thou mayst not wander in that labyrinth.

145   There Minotaurs and ugly treasons lurk.

146   Solicit Henry with her wondrous praise.

    Bethink thee on her virtues that surmount,

148   Mad natural graces that extinguish art.

149   Repeat their semblance often on the seas,

150   That when thou com'st to kneel at Henry's feet

151   Thou mayst bereave him of his wits with wonder.

                                             Exeunt.

*

❧ **V.6** *Enter Richard Duke of York, the Earl of Warwick, and a Shepherd.*

RICHARD DUKE OF YORK

    Bring forth that sorceress condemned to burn.

    Enter Joan la Pucelle, guarded.

SHEPHERD

    Ah, Joan, this kills thy father's heart outright.

3   Have I sought every country far and near,

4   And now it is my chance to find thee out

5   Must I behold thy timeless cruel death?

    Ah Joan, sweet daughter Joan, I'll die with thee.

JOAN

7   Decrepit miser, base ignoble wretch,

---

142 *peevish* trifling   145 *Minotaurs* (there was but one Minotaur, a monster part bull and part man, at the center of the Cretan labyrinth built by Daedalus)   146 *Solicit* entice; *her wondrous praise* praise of this wondrous woman   148 *Mad* extravagant; *extinguish* eclipse   149 *Repeat their semblance* rehearse the description of her virtues   151 *bereave* dispossess

    V.6 The Duke of York's camp, France   3 *sought* searched   4 *find thee out* discover you   5 *timeless* premature   7 *miser* wretch

I am descended of a gentler blood.   8
Thou art no father nor no friend of mine.   9

SHEPHERD
Out, out! – My lords, an't please you, 'tis not so.   10
I did beget her, all the parish knows.
Her mother liveth yet, can testify
She was the first fruit of my bach'lorship.

WARWICK   *To Joan*
Graceless, wilt thou deny thy parentage?   14

RICHARD DUKE OF YORK
This argues what her kind of life hath been –   15
Wicked and vile; and so her death concludes.   16

SHEPHERD
Fie, Joan, that thou wilt be so obstacle.   17
God knows thou art a collop of my flesh,   18
And for thy sake have I shed many a tear.
Deny me not, I prithee, gentle Joan.   20

JOAN
Peasant, avaunt! *(To the English)* You have suborned this
   man
Of purpose to obscure my noble birth.

SHEPHERD   *To the English*
'Tis true I gave a noble to the priest   23
The morn that I was wedded to her mother.
   To Joan
Kneel down, and take my blessing, good my girl.
Wilt thou not stoop? Now cursèd be the time
Of thy nativity. I would the milk
Thy mother gave thee when thou sucked'st her breast
Had been a little ratsbane for thy sake.   29
Or else, when thou didst keep my lambs afield,   30
I wish some ravenous wolf had eaten thee.

---

8 *gentler* better bred, more aristocratic   9 *friend* kinsman   14 *Graceless* depraved person   15 *argues* testifies to   16 *concludes* (1) verifies, (2) ends   17 *obstacle* (he means to say "obstinate")   18 *collop* slice   23 *noble* coin worth about one third of a pound   29 *ratsbane* rat poison   30 *keep* tend

32   Dost thou deny thy father, cursèd drab?
            To the English
        O burn her, burn her! Hanging is too good.   *Exit.*
    RICHARD DUKE OF YORK   *To the Guards*
        Take her away, for she hath lived too long,
        To fill the world with vicious qualities.
    JOAN
        First let me tell you whom you have condemned:
        Not one begotten of a shepherd swain,
        But issued from the progeny of kings;
        Virtuous and holy, chosen from above
40   By inspiration of celestial grace
41   To work exceeding miracles on earth.
        I never had to do with wicked spirits;
        But you that are polluted with your lusts,
        Stained with the guiltless blood of innocents,
        Corrupt and tainted with a thousand vices –
46   Because you want the grace that others have,
47   You judge it straight a thing impossible
48   To compass wonders but by help of devils.
        No, misconceivèd Joan of Arc hath been
50   A virgin from her tender infancy,
        Chaste and immaculate in very thought,
52   Whose maiden blood thus rigorously effused
        Will cry for vengeance at the gates of heaven.
    RICHARD DUKE OF YORK
        Ay, ay, *(To the Guards)* away with her to execution.
    WARWICK   *To the Guards*
        And hark ye, sirs: because she is a maid,
        Spare for no faggots. Let there be enough.
        Place barrels of pitch upon the fatal stake,
        That so her torture may be shortenèd.

------

32 *drab* whore   41 *exceeding* exceptional   46 *want* lack   47 *straight* immediately   48 *compass* accomplish   52 *rigorously effused* cruelly shed

JOAN

  Will nothing turn your unrelenting hearts?   59

  Then Joan, discover thine infirmity,   60

  That warranteth by law to be thy privilege:

  I am with child, ye bloody homicides.

  Murder not then the fruit within my womb,

  Although ye hale me to a violent death.   64

RICHARD DUKE OF YORK

  Now heaven forfend – the holy maid with child?   65

WARWICK   *To Joan*

  The greatest miracle that e'er ye wrought.

  Is all your strict preciseness come to this?   67

RICHARD DUKE OF YORK

  She and the dauphin have been ingling.   68

  I did imagine what would be her refuge.   69

WARWICK

  Well, go to, we will have no bastards live,   70

  Especially since Charles must father it.

JOAN

  You are deceived. My child is none of his.

  It was Alençon that enjoyed my love.

RICHARD DUKE OF YORK

  Alençon, that notorious Machiavel?   74

  It dies an if it had a thousand lives.

JOAN

  O give me leave, I have deluded you.

  'Twas neither Charles nor yet the duke I named,

  But René King of Naples that prevailed.

WARWICK

  A married man? – That's most intolerable.

---

59 *turn* change 60 *discover* reveal 64 *hale* drag 65 *forfend* forbid 67 *preciseness* propriety 68 *ingling* having sex, dallying 69 *imagine* wonder; *refuge* last defense 74 *Machiavel* Niccolò Machiavelli (1469–1572), the Italian writer and statesman whose doctrines Elizabethans regarded as the epitome of intrigue and immoral expediency

RICHARD DUKE OF YORK

80   Why, here's a girl; I think she knows not well –
     There were so many – whom she may accuse.

WARWICK

82   It's sign she hath been liberal and free.

RICHARD DUKE OF YORK
     And yet forsooth she is a virgin pure!
          To Joan
     Strumpet, thy words condemn thy brat and thee.
     Use no entreaty, for it is in vain.

JOAN
     Then lead me hence; with whom I leave my curse.

87   May never glorious sun reflex his beams
     Upon the country where you make abode,
     But darkness and the gloomy shade of death

90   Environ you till mischief and despair
     Drive you to break your necks or hang yourselves.
          Enter the Cardinal of Winchester.

RICHARD DUKE OF YORK   *To Joan*

92   Break thou in pieces, and consume to ashes,
     Thou foul accursèd minister of hell.

                              Exit Joan, guarded.

CARDINAL OF WINCHESTER
     Lord Regent, I do greet your excellence
     With letters of commission from the king.
     For know, my lords, the states of Christendom,

97   Moved with remorse of these outrageous broils,
     Have earnestly implored a general peace
     Betwixt our nation and the aspiring French,

100 And here at hand the dauphin and his train
     Approacheth to confer about some matter.

RICHARD DUKE OF YORK

102 Is all our travail turned to this effect?

---

82 *liberal* (1) generous, (2) promiscuous   **87** *reflex* throw   **90** *mischief* mis-
fortune   **92** *consume* burn up entirely   **97** *remorse of* pity for   **102** *travail*
toil

After the slaughter of so many peers,
So many captains, gentlemen, and soldiers
That in this quarrel have been overthrown
And sold their bodies for their country's benefit,
Shall we at last conclude effeminate peace?
Have we not lost most part of all the towns
By treason, falsehood, and by treachery,
Our great progenitors had conquerèd?   *110*
O Warwick, Warwick, I foresee with grief
The utter loss of all the realm of France!

WARWICK
Be patient, York. If we conclude a peace
It shall be with such strict and severe covenants   *114*
As little shall the Frenchmen gain thereby.   *115*
    Enter Charles the Dauphin, the Duke of Alençon,
    the Bastard of Orléans, and René Duke of Anjou.

CHARLES
Since, lords of England, it is thus agreed
That peaceful truce shall be proclaimed in France,
We come to be informèd by yourselves
What the conditions of that league must be.   *119*

RICHARD DUKE OF YORK   *To Winchester*
Speak, Winchester; for boiling choler chokes   *120*
The hollow passage of my poisoned voice
By sight of these our baleful enemies.   *122*

CARDINAL OF WINCHESTER
Charles and the rest, it is enacted thus:
That, in regard King Henry gives consent,   *124*
Of mere compassion and of lenity,   *125*
To ease your country of distressful war
And suffer you to breathe in fruitful peace,   *127*
You shall become true liegemen to his crown.
And, Charles, upon condition thou wilt swear

---

114 *covenants* articles of agreement 115 *As* that 119 *league* treaty 120
choler anger 122 *baleful* deadly 124 *in regard* inasmuch as 125 *mere*
pure; *lenity* mercifulness 127 *suffer* allow

130   To pay him tribute and submit thyself,
       Thou shalt be placed as viceroy under him,
       And still enjoy thy regal dignity.

ALENÇON
       Must he be then as shadow of himself? –
       Adorn his temples with a coronet,
       And yet in substance and authority
       Retain but privilege of a private man?
       This proffer is absurd and reasonless.

CHARLES
       'Tis known already that I am possessed
139   With more than half the Gallian territories,
140   And therein reverenced for their lawful king.
141   Shall I, for lucre of the rest unvanquished,
       Detract so much from that prerogative
143   As to be called but viceroy of the whole?
       No, Lord Ambassador, I'll rather keep
       That which I have than, coveting for more,
146   Be cast from possibility of all.

RICHARD DUKE OF YORK
       Insulting Charles, hast thou by secret means
       Used intercession to obtain a league
149   And, now the matter grows to compromise,
150   Stand'st thou aloof upon comparison?
       Either accept the title thou usurp'st,
152   Of benefit proceeding from our king
153   And not of any challenge of desert,
       Or we will plague thee with incessant wars.

RENÉ   *Aside to Charles*
       My lord, you do not well in obstinacy
       To cavil in the course of this contract.
157   If once it be neglected, ten to one

---

139 *Gallian* French   141 *lucre* profit; *rest* rest that are   143 *but* merely   146 *cast* excluded   149 *grows to compromise* approaches a peaceful solution   150 *comparison* rhetorical quibbling   152 *Of benefit* as feudal beneficiary   153 *challenge of desert* claim of right to the title   157 *neglected* disregarded

We shall not find like opportunity.
ALENÇON   *Aside to Charles*
  To say the truth, it is your policy   159
  To save your subjects from such massacre   *160*
  And ruthless slaughters as are daily seen
  By our proceeding in hostility;
  And therefore take this compact of a truce,
  Although you break it when your pleasure serves.
WARWICK
  How sayst thou, Charles? Shall our condition stand?   165
CHARLES
  It shall,
  Only reserved you claim no interest   167
  In any of our towns of garrison.   168
RICHARD DUKE OF YORK
  Then swear allegiance to his majesty,
  As thou art knight, never to disobey   *170*
  Nor be rebellious to the crown of England,
  Thou nor thy nobles, to the crown of England.
    They swear.
  So, now dismiss your army when ye please.
  Hang up your ensigns, let your drums be still;
  For here we entertain a solemn peace.   *Exeunt.*

*

∾ **V.7** *Enter the Earl of Suffolk, in conference with King*
    Henry, and the Dukes of Gloucester and Exeter.

KING HENRY   *To Suffolk*
  Your wondrous rare description, noble earl,
  Of beauteous Margaret hath astonished me.
  Her virtues gracèd with external gifts
  Do breed love's settled passions in my heart,   4

---

159 *policy* politic course   165 *condition* treaty terms   167 *Only reserved* with
the sole reservation that   168 *towns of garrison* fortified towns
  V.7 The palace, London   4 *settled* rooted

5   And like as rigor of tempestuous gusts
6   Provokes the mightiest hulk against the tide,
7   So am I driven by breath of her renown
     Either to suffer shipwreck or arrive
     Where I may have fruition of her love.

SUFFOLK
10   Tush, my good lord, this superficial tale
11   Is but a preface of her worthy praise.
     The chief perfections of that lovely dame,
     Had I sufficient skill to utter them,
     Would make a volume of enticing lines
15   Able to ravish any dull conceit;
     And, which is more, she is not so divine,
17   So full replete with choice of all delights,
     But with as humble lowliness of mind
     She is content to be at your command –
20   Command, I mean, of virtuous chaste intents,
     To love and honor Henry as her lord.

KING HENRY
     And otherwise will Henry ne'er presume.
      To Gloucester
     Therefore, my Lord Protector, give consent
     That Marg'ret may be England's royal queen.

GLOUCESTER
25   So should I give consent to flatter sin.
     You know, my lord, your highness is betrothed
     Unto another lady of esteem.
     How shall we then dispense with that contract
     And not deface your honor with reproach?

SUFFOLK
30   As doth a ruler with unlawful oaths,
31   Or one that, at a triumph having vowed

---

5 *rigor* violent force 6 *Provokes* impels; *hulk* ship 7 *renown* famous reputation 10 *superficial* dealing merely with her most obvious virtues 11 *her worthy praise* the praise she deserves 15 *conceit* imagination 17 *full* fully 25 *flatter* extenuate 31 *triumph* tournament

To try his strength, forsaketh yet the lists   32
By reason of his adversary's odds.
A poor earl's daughter is unequal odds,
And therefore may be broke without offense.

GLOUCESTER
Why, what, I pray, is Margaret more than that?
Her father is no better than an earl,
Although in glorious titles he excel.

SUFFOLK
Yes, my lord; her father is a king,
The King of Naples and Jerusalem,   40
And of such great authority in France
As his alliance will confirm our peace
And keep the Frenchmen in allegiance.

GLOUCESTER
And so the Earl of Armagnac may do,
Because he is near kinsman unto Charles.

EXETER
Beside, his wealth doth warrant a liberal dower,   46
Where René sooner will receive than give.

SUFFOLK
A dower, my lords? Disgrace not so your king
That he should be so abject, base, and poor
To choose for wealth and not for perfect love.   50
Henry is able to enrich his queen,
And not to seek a queen to make him rich.
So worthless peasants bargain for their wives,
As marketmen for oxen, sheep, or horse.
Marriage is a matter of more worth
Than to be dealt in by attorneyship.   56
Not whom *we* will but whom his grace affects   57
Must be companion of his nuptial bed.
And therefore, lords, since he affects her most,
That most of all these reasons bindeth us: 60

---

32 *lists* tilting area at a tournament   **46** *warrant* guarantee   **56** *attorneyship*
proxy   **57** *affects* desires

In our opinions she should be preferred.
62 For what is wedlock forcèd but a hell,
An age of discord and continual strife,
Whereas the contrary bringeth bliss,
65 And is a pattern of celestial peace.
Whom should we match with Henry, being a king,
But Margaret, that is daughter to a king?
68 Her peerless feature joinèd with her birth
69 Approves her fit for none but for a king.
70 Her valiant courage and undaunted spirit,
More than in women commonly is seen,
Will answer our hope in issue of a king.
For Henry, son unto a conqueror,
Is likely to beget more conquerors
75 If with a lady of so high resolve
As is fair Margaret he be linked in love.
Then yield, my lords, and here conclude with me:
That Margaret shall be queen, and none but she.

KING HENRY
Whether it be through force of your report,
80 My noble Lord of Suffolk, or for that
81 My tender youth was never yet attaint
With any passion of inflaming love,
I cannot tell; but this I am assured:
I feel such sharp dissension in my breast,
Such fierce alarums both of hope and fear,
As I am sick with working of my thoughts.
87 Take therefore shipping; post, my lord, to France;
Agree to any covenants, and procure
89 That Lady Margaret do vouchsafe to come
90 To cross the seas to England and be crowned
King Henry's faithful and anointed queen.

---

62 *wedlock forcèd* enforced marriage   65 *pattern* example   68 *feature* form;
birth high rank   69 *Approves her* confirms that she is   75 *resolve* determination   80 *for that* because   81 *attaint* diseased   87 *post* hurry   89 *vouchsafe*
promise

For your expenses and sufficient charge,   92
Among the people gather up a tenth.   93
Be gone, I say; for till you do return
I rest perplexèd with a thousand cares.   95
    To Gloucester
And you, good uncle, banish all offense.   96
If you do censure me by what you were,   97
Not what you are, I know it will excuse
This sudden execution of my will.
And so conduct me where from company   100
I may revolve and ruminate my grief.   *Exit with Exeter.*
GLOUCESTER
    Ay, grief, I fear me, both at first and last.   *Exit.*
SUFFOLK
    Thus Suffolk hath prevailed, and thus he goes
    As did the youthful Paris once to Greece,   104
    With hope to find the like event in love,   105
    But prosper better than the Trojan did.
    Margaret shall now be queen and rule the king;
    But I will rule both her, the king, and realm.   *Exit.*

---

92 *charge* money to spend   93 *a tenth* ten percent of value of personal property appropriated as tax   95 *rest* remain   96 *offense* hostility   97–98 *censure . . . are* i.e., measure my proposed extravagances by the libertinism of your own youth, not by the gravity of your present age   100 *from company* alone   104 *Paris* son of King Priam of Troy (Paris's abduction of Helen, wife of King Menelaus of Sparta, led to the Trojan War)   105 *event* outcome (i.e., Paris's winning of Helen)

The distinguished Pelican Shakespeare series, newly revised
to be the premier choice for students, professors, and
general readers well into the 21st century

FOR THE BEST IN PAPERBACKS, LOOK FOR THE

In every corner of the world, on every subject under the sun, Penguin represents quality and variety—the very best in publishing today.

For complete information about books available from Penguin—including Puffins, Penguin Classics, and Arkana—and how to order them, write to us at the appropriate address below. Please note that for copyright reasons the selection of books varies from country to country.

In the United Kingdom: Please write to *Dept. EP, Penguin Books Ltd, Bath Road, Harmondsworth, West Drayton, Middlesex UB7 0DA.*

In the United States: Please write to *Penguin Putnam Inc., P.O. Box 12289 Dept. B, Newark, New Jersey 07101-5289* or call *1-800-788-6262.*

In Canada: Please write to *Penguin Books Canada Ltd, 10 Alcorn Avenue, Suite 300, Toronto, Ontario M4V 3B2.*

In Australia: Please write to *Penguin Books Australia Ltd, P.O. Box 257, Ringwood, Victoria 3134.*

In New Zealand: Please write to *Penguin Books (NZ) Ltd, Private Bag 102902, North Shore Mail Centre, Auckland 10.*

In India: Please write to *Penguin Books India Pvt Ltd, 11 Panchsheel Shopping Centre, Panchsheel Park, New Delhi 110 017.*

In the Netherlands: Please write to *Penguin Books Netherlands bv, Postbus 3507, NL-1001 AH Amsterdam.*

In Germany: Please write to *Penguin Books Deutschland GmbH, Metzlerstrasse 26, 60594 Frankfurt am Main.*

In Spain: Please write to *Penguin Books S. A., Bravo Murillo 19, 1° B, 28015 Madrid.*

In Italy: Please write to *Penguin Italia s.r.l., Via Benedetto Croce 2, 20094 Corsico, Milano.*

In France: Please write to *Penguin France, Le Carré Wilson, 62 rue Benjamin Baillaud, 31500 Toulouse.*

In Japan: Please write to *Penguin Books Japan Ltd, Kaneko Building, 2-3-25 Koraku, Bunkyo-Ku, Tokyo 112.*

In South Africa: Please write to *Penguin Books South Africa (Pty) Ltd, Private Bag X14, Parkview, 2122 Johannesburg.*